A Guide for the Family Therapist

A Guide
for the
Family Therapist

Patricia A. Boyer
Ronnald J. Jeffrey

with Karen Schoenhals

JASON ARONSON INC.
Northvale, New Jersey
London

THE ILLUSTRATOR

Helmut J. Anderson, MSW, is director of the Sweetwater County Department of Public Assistance and Social Services. He began work with the state of Wyoming as a caseworker in Sweetwater County in 1968 and has held a variety of positions in social work. He has always been interested in art and greatly enjoys any opportunity that helps combine social work with art—as a way of illustrating concepts, or counseling situations, or just plain poking fun.

This book was previously published under state grant 76A-25-810 as *The Family: A Living Kaleidoscope*.

THE MASTER WORK SERIES

First softcover edition 1994

Library of Congress Cataloging-in-Publication Data

ISBN: 1-56821-285-2
Library of Congress Catalog Card Number: 83-3799

Manufactured in the United States of America. Jason Aronson Inc. offers books and cassettes. For information and catalog write to Jason Aronson Inc., 230 Livingston Street, Northvale, New Jersey 07647.

To Marilyn and Keeya
and to Clair—
who endured, encouraged, inspired, shared,
and, most of all, loved.

Contents

Foreword

The approach to the important area of family therapy in this book is used by community-based crisis intervention teams in many types of institutions: psychiatric hospitals, emergency rooms, juvenile halls, and jails. This use reflects a shift in focus within the mental health field, from one-to-one therapy between the therapist and an individual client to an interest in group therapy, family therapy, multiple family therapy, network therapy, and industrial workplace therapy.

As families have become smaller and individuals more isolated in our mobile society, many former support systems have been lost. Crisis intervention was once the territory of the older, more experienced members of an extended family: parents consulted their own parents or grandparents for advice, and children were taken in by helpful relatives in times of stress. The "cop on the block," the family doctor, and the neighborhood clergy augmented the family's experience and provided an outside authority when necessary. Group or family counseling has developed in response to the needs of individuals who have found themselves without the support that family and neighborhood once provided during a crisis.

In addition, the practice of removing people from home and community to distant institutions, from which the return home is difficult, has lost favor within the helping professions. We assume, as do the authors, that both the individual and the group have certain strengths that can be mobilized at times of stress, both large and small, which is a part of daily living. At times stress is so great that agencies and professionals are sought, with the purpose of strengthening the family rather than further isolating the individual with a problem.

This is particularly true when the person in trouble is a child. If the family can be taught to be more effective, closer, and more supportive, everyone benefits; if the child's behavior is viewed as a barometer of stormy times in the family, other problems may come to light and be dealt with as part of the child's context of living. As this book demonstrates, it is possible to detect and interrupt repeated patterns that impede the child's and family's growth and development.

Based on their personal clinical experience, the authors have written this book to present their way of working. They treat the reader as a trusted colleague, providing rich case examples that demonstrate their understanding of family counseling. Their own brand of warmth and commitment emerges as they explain, lecture, describe their experience, and provide many practical guidelines.

Boyer and Jeffrey are enthusiastic, helpful, sometimes even lyrical representatives of their craft. Their book offers a chance for a friendly consultation with experts who remember their own beginnings and find ways to elucidate their encounters with troubled families.

Alan Leveton, M.D.
Eva Leveton, M.S.
Family Therapy Center, San Francisco

Preface

This book is about families — their joys and pains, happiness and sorrows. No other unit in society is more responsible for the healthy growth of a person, because it is through a family's development of healthy interactional patterns that its members gain a perspective of who they are, what they are, and what they might become. This book is about people who are members of families and for people who are involved in helping them. It is about relationships between husbands and wives, parents and children, brothers and sisters, counselors and clients.

The book was written primarily for human service workers with basic backgrounds in counseling but with limited experience in working with entire families. It is not designed to teach family therapy techniques, though techniques are discussed. Techniques cannot be taught; they can only be shared. We share ideas, techniques, and beliefs, not as absolutes, but as "another way" or "a different thought" that readers might incorporate into their personal style of helping.

This book is an outgrowth of our training at the Cheyenne Office of Youth Alternatives, which was awarded a two-year training grant in 1977 from the Governor's Planning Committee on Criminal Administration to improve family counseling skills of human service workers in the field of corrections. We worked with recognized authorities in the field of family therapy to develop and present the training program. Training was conducted in three phases: Phase I, Theoretical Orientation; Phase II, Skill Development; and Phase III, Consultation and Follow-up. Though we had practiced family therapy independently, writing the book and conducting the training offered us an opportunity to work together, and to share ideas and see them grow. Through the workshops our ideas were tested and refined.

We describe our experiences in family counseling and borrow from the work and writings of a number of highly skilled family therapists. Ideas have been intermingled to produce an approach to dealing with problems in family relationships that has proved helpful and workable.

Acknowledgments

Karen Schoenhals, R.N., M.A., a psychiatric nurse, was a major contributor to the development of this book. She was primarily responsible for writing Chapter 1 and provided assistance with the entire book. Her creative energy brought us the theme of the kaleidoscope throughout the book, and her sharing of knowledge, time, and ideas was a tremendous asset in working on the book.

The completion of the book was made possible through the generous sharing of ideas and concepts by many individuals — family members, students, colleagues, friends, and other people. Special thanks are due Sherry Welch, Jim Lucero, and the rest of the staff of the Office of Youth Alternatives, and Cecilia Rogers and Brad Bauer for sharing their experiences. The authors also are grateful to Mary Woolsey for her generous editorial support.

1
DEFINITION OF A FAMILY

The family sat together in front of the glowing fireplace. It was Christmas Day with the familiar air of excitement and the luscious odors of Christmas dinner cooking in the kitchen. A kaleidoscope, brought earlier by Santa and placed in a huge handknit stocking, was the focus of the family's attention. Each family member in turn gazed in awe through the aperture at the end of the rotating tube, experiencing an exquisite array of constantly changing symmetrical designs of bright colors reflecting on the background of mirrors. No two patterns were alike. With a slight rotation of the tube, one pattern was gone forever while another, equally unique, appeared.

What is a "family"? The term is difficult to define since it embraces a tremendous range of characteristics, behaviors, functions, and experiences. A family is an ever-changing series of relationships — an active, forceful, and growing artistic design that delicately integrates human needs. A family is a continually changing pattern of brilliant and less distinct hues as its members move within their individual frameworks, with each juxtaposed component affected, inspired, and helped by the others. A family is like a living kaleidoscope (Fig. 1) made up of unique personalities relating to other unique personalities. A family might be considered an artistic creation which, when viewed from different angles, projects both characteristic and divergent patterns.

John Donne said, "no man is an island," meaning that man does not exist as an isolate. People are dependent on living cooperatively within the structure of a group to survive. The family is society's primary social group, the very foundation in which individuals have their beginnings and through which they experience the major portion of life.

The family is a group of people living intimately together as a unit, sharing life's anticipations, disappointments, struggles, and

1

Figure 1. The family is like a living kaleidoscope made up of unique personalities relating to other unique personalities.

joys. Complex communication skills connect unique individuals as the family grows and develops cohesiveness.

The family must shoulder the pressures of modern-day living and, simultaneously, must be responsible for meeting the individual and mutually shared needs of its members, who, because they are at different stages of development, have unique goals that must be reached if each member is to realize his or her potential. At times, an individual family member's personal needs may collide with the needs of the total group. Although this can be a cause of stress to both individual and group, it must not be allowed to disrupt the family process if the unit is to achieve its task of developing potential. As individual family members strive to see their personal potential become fact, the family, as a unit, is also engaged in a developmental struggle.

Laura Dodson (1978) stated, "These dual, sometimes contrasting, human needs create the paradoxes of the family unit, in which exist struggle for separateness and togetherness, differentness and sameness, protection and freedom, support and independence." Human beings fail to thrive physically, emotionally, intellectually, and spiritually if they do not have the healthy balance of the family environment in which to develop.

As each member of a family interacts on a one-to-one basis with each other family member, each individual's expectations dictate, to some extent, the behavior of other members. At the same time, each member plays out his or her designated social role, which is a person's relationship with other members as established by society, that dictates specifying the expectations and functions of each member within the group. Roles provide a necessary sense of structure within a family relationship, but today's social roles create a confusing kaleidoscopic clash because each person is struggling to achieve individuality while, at the same time, meeting the expectations of their role. Conflict develops in relationships when a person's individual identity is contrary to role expectations. Therefore, some of the attention of a family therapist focuses on helping individuals find themselves as they move in and out of the role-prescribed patterns within the family.

Virginia Satir (1967) states that "The marital relationship is the axis around which all family relationships are formed. The mates are the architects of the family." A hierarchy of leadership must be created within the family structure in which individuals, according to their roles within the family, have differing levels of authority and responsibility. Satir's statement implies that the parents, in a complementary and cooperative fashion, assume the leadership role in establishing boundaries between parents and offspring to protect, preserve, and maintain the essential leadership function. Salvador Minuchin (1974) points out that a new family unit begins formally when two partners join with the express intent of forming a family. He says that in order for a family to operate effectively, there must be cohesiveness between the mates as well as clear-cut, well-defined generational boundaries. This allows members to function in their roles without interference, thus maintaining a state of equilibrium with the family.

Increasingly, family therapists are discovering that where kaleidoscopic patterns within a family lose their symmetry and hues begin to clash, a lack of harmony exists between the husband and wife. Complications within a family often arise when the partners come together when they are still maturing and bring with them unresolved past experiences as family members. The newly formed family unit may well have difficulty integrating the values, beliefs, and traditions of each mate's family of origin under the circumstances. The resulting disharmony is accompanied by confusion of interactional patterns and a breakdown of leadership functions.

The family system carries out its basic functions through ever-changing subdivisions within the group. The smaller groups are referred to as dyads and triads, the ebb and flow between which are dictated by situation and need. Interdependent relationships exist among the dyads and triads as each member influences the experiences, feelings, and perceptions of other members. Individuals enter into temporary coalitions designed to serve various different purposes, such as protection or achieving goals. Unfortunately, some partnerships can be destructive to the family's interaction.

The family therapist should always be cognizant of the potentially destructive influence of fixed alliance between members within the family structure. Dyads and triads in healthy families constantly change as individuals are called upon to flow in and out of relationships according to the demands of circumstances, needs, and desires.

Physiologically, all living organisms possess a system that automatically compensates to counteract imbalances. When a state of disequilibrium exists, the state itself motivates the organism to correct the imbalance. Considered as a living organism, a family structure can be said to have homeostatic devices to maintain a state of equilibrium. When one component functions ineffectively, the total system suffers, and so families strive constantly to maintain an internal balance, even to the extreme of healthy members compensating for the malfunctioning of another member. Individual members fit into a predictable pattern as each one constantly adapts behavior in accordance with the actions of other family members. One member's action creates a corresponding reaction that is comfortable to the total family group, even if dysfunctional, because it fits into a known pattern and maintains family balance.

Human beings need order in their universe to create a feeling of certainty; likewise, they need to control and balance family dynamics to provide feelings of security and predictability. This balance is achieved through "family rules" or the kaleidoscopic code. Each family has a unique set of rules which, according to Dodson (1978), may be defined as "non-verbally agreed-upon behaviors that usually are implied rather than explicitly stated and are frequently outside the awareness of the family members." The rules constitute each family's unique kaleidoscopic code through which is organized, dictated, and defined the manner in which family members relate and interact.

Designed to preclude direct conflict and maintain balance, the kaleidoscopic code regulates the behavior and expectations of the group. The intricate balance of the group depends upon each individual's willingness or ability to live by the code. Once patterns are established, each member must constantly (though unconsciously) decide whether to conform, rebel, or create new patterns. When equilibrium is not present, family members experience stress and are motivated to adapt their conduct to the prescribed expectations of the group; thus the family uses special homeostatic devices to maintain balance. Even though a family might maintain balance, however, its dynamics may not be healthy. Often dysfunctional codes are established, and though they prevent direct confrontation, emotional growth is inhibited and the family prevented from becoming a truly effective unit.

An example from nature illustrates the point. If sunlight is blocked, a flower will bend and twist until it reaches the growth-enhancing rays. So too do some families go through a process, often painful and dysfunctional, of bending and twisting to maintain balance, even when such balance is achieved through dysfunctional interactional patterns that cause emotional pain and heartache for the members.

We might like to picture the family in a stereotyped sense as a kaleidoscopic image locked in place in a traditional design — symmetrical, harmonious, balanced. The nuclear family most nearly fits these criteria with its intact bonds, impenetrable boundaries, and blended hues of complementary colors. Born out of a romantic burst of expectation and hope, this primary unit of society consists of mother, father, and their biological or adopted offspring. The design is integrated and structured, and the members experience a feeling of permanence and security. Usually, both parents have an equal bond with the children since both have direct responsibility for and legal rights to the children.

Unexpected events, however, do arise — disasters, deaths, divorces. These events rock the family and, as with the rotating of the kaleidoscope, a new family constellation appears, while the old one is gone forever. The family pattern changes, an important component is missing, and the design loses its symmetry. The single-parent family emerges with its members struggling to find their places in a pattern that has drastically changed. Children in divorced families live with a custodial parent and have another biological parent living outside the family. The children pass between and penetrate the patterns of two households. Because leadership responsibility often shifts from parent to child in one-parent households, all members experience role confusion at times.

In many cases, the single-parent family is only a transitional unit as the parent begins courting and possibly considering remarriage. Attempting to come to terms with the reality that their parents will not get back together places a strain on the children. When the single parent remarries and a new family, a "step-family," evolves, attempts are made to establish a balance in the new family. Chaos, feelings of uncertainty and insecurity, and frequent changes in the kaleidoscopic constellation tinge the complexion of the newly developed design. As John and Emily Visher (1979) stated in their book *Step-Families*, "There is often a sense of impermanence to the step-family relationship, a factor which can threaten the feeling of security of all members."

Although a step-family appears similar to a nuclear family, there are many significant differences. In the step-family one of the parents is not a biological parent, and regardless of whether the absent natural parent is dead or missing due to divorce, feelings of separation and loss dominate the new pattern. At the time the new family unit is being formed, feelings of resentment and competition may occur, especially in the children, preventing the family from bonding as a unit. Moreover, the original locked-in kaleidoscopic design that embraces the natural parent and the children predates the new marital relationship. The two parents are thus at different emotional stages in their relationship with the children, and conflict between the spouses often is created. The biological parent may feel threatened and might even resist a step-parent's efforts to initiate a parent–child bond; thus, the emerging family pattern may suffer a lack of balance.

Alternative family patterns are now challenging family therapists. A therapist today is required to have a sophisticated understanding of family dynamics and the ability to vary therapeutic approaches according to specific family structures. Within the confines of its structure, the family serves many functions essential both to the definition of the family and to the growth and development of human beings. Family experience is essential to turn uninhibited newborn infants into full-functioning human beings with a sense of identity — individuals with values, beliefs, and standards, people who possess the ability to live harmoniously with others. Regardless of the type of structure, the family has the basic and all-encompassing function to produce young adults capable of living well-adjusted and productive lives.

According to Salvador Minuchin (1974), the family is the matrix of self-identity, and family experience is at the very core of self-knowledge. Interacting within the subsystems of the family structure, the child discovers who he or she is as an individual in relation to others. As part of the process of self-definition, the child develops the essential sense of belonging and the crucial sense of being a separate and unique individual. Concurrently, the child gains a sense of self-esteem within the family.

Self-esteem is built on the self-concept reinforcement messages the child receives or perceives in interacting with other family members. A child's interactions with other social groups augment feelings of identity and self-worth as he or she grows older, but the basis of self-value comes from family experiences. Satir (1972) states: "Feelings of worth flourish in an atmosphere that allows for self-expression, tolerance of differences and in an atmosphere that is open and flexible."

How to conduct human relationships is also learned in the family. One is constantly involved in human relationships: people must always react or respond to other people. It is within the confines of primary relationships, however, that children learn how to interact and negotiate effectively. Characteristics such as loyalty, dependability, trustworthiness, compassion, sensitivity to others, thoughtfulness, and unselfishness have their roots within the family, as does the ability to accept the importance and significance of other people. All of these traits are essential in human relationships. These positive characteristics do not appear automatically. Someone must take time and energy to instill these values in children as they grow and develop.

Communication is learned in the family environment. An infant is not born with the ability to communicate. Babies do not have the skills needed to interact with other people. Children must learn to communicate through the long process of interacting with parents and other family members. In addition, children first learn within the family environment to communicate on a peer level as well as to communicate effectively in situations where they lack equal status and power.

The family is an economic unit, the center where children learn the significance of money and how to manage financial affairs. Children learn to establish priorities for spending money when they are included in discussions about the financial position and concerns of the family. As a member of the family, the child learns to set aside personal desires in favor of a higher priority of another family member. The child learns to give, to receive, and to sacrifice. Just as important, the child learns to be the recipient of another member's sacrifices.

The family may be viewed as an educational unit in which cultural concerns and traditions are transmitted from one generation to the next. Each parent contributes a cultural heritage and unique family customs to be passed on to offspring. Parents are thus committed to the stimulating mission of sharing with their children ancestral information vital to their sense of identity.

The family holds a tremendous responsibility in the formal education of its children, for within the family, basic attitudes toward learning develop. The educational system can provide an academic curriculum, but the family's influence often determines whether a child takes advantage of educational opportunities. Parents, in essence, are responsible for overseeing, enhancing, augmenting, and filtering the total education of their children, intellectually, spiritually, culturally, and emotionally.

The family provides the environment in which human beings may grow and become. Ideally, the family serves as a refuge from problems, attacks, and anxieties that individual members face daily. The atmosphere within the family gives each member permission to shed social masks and truly be him- or herself. The family thus provides comfort and encouragement to enable members to meet their fullest potential.

The family is a microcosm of society, the most important segment of society, the very cradle of human nature. This introductory chapter touches only the surface of all a family is and can be. The possible number of kaleidoscopic components and patterns are too numerous to consider in this brief overview. This chapter introduces the family in an ideal fashion where there is sufficient light to see the beautiful array of patterns and where the hues and shapes of the individual pieces are in a complementary relationship. In reality, the family seldom fits the ideal pattern. Sometimes family dynamics do not yield beautiful designs. Sometimes there is insufficient light to see the patterns. Sometimes the individual colors and shapes clash, preventing harmony within the constellation.

In general, the family today is a neglected group whose interrelated processes and ability to function effectively are taken for granted. Energies are invested, instead, in all kinds of outside activities, including careers, education, and community projects. Recognizing the significance of the family and investing energy into its well-being constitute the most important challenge of our age. To this end, this text is dedicated to the development of beginning family therapists who will invest time, energy, and skills in helping families *grow, develop,* and *become.*

2
AN HISTORICAL PERSPECTIVE

Twenty-five years ago it was virtually inconceivable that relationship problems would be discussed with the entire family present. Because the first contact in therapy with people in crisis was on an individual basis, problems in interpersonal relationships were generally viewed as emanating from within the person. Therapy consisted of a series of conversations between the therapist and the client about the client's thoughts, feelings, and earlier life experiences, with the hope of gaining insight, understanding, and, ultimately, change. Minimal attention was given to the fact that a person's pain was both a cause and a product of psychological and emotional pain within the family or to the idea that actions and reactions of others close to a person might shape that person's behavior.

Counselors, social workers, and therapists who made home visits frequently were blind to one of Nature's most basic laws: that all life, from the simplest to the most complex, is interwoven with varying degrees of interdependence—that when you stub your toes the body limps, that when part of the whole is weakened the whole, in fact, is weakened.

An awakening to this fact (Fig. 2) provided the impetus for major changes in counseling and psychotherapy, as human service practitioners across the country became increasingly dissatisfied with the limited success of "one-to-one" therapy in dealing with family and marital problems. Pioneers in family therapy struggled to free themselves from the traditional ideology that required concentrating strictly on the individual, researching and validating their beliefs during the 1950s.

Gregory Bateson (1956) and his associates in Palo Alto, California, for instance, conducted a research project to study the relationship between schizophrenia and interpersonal communication patterns. The study strongly suggested that certain behaviors manifested by people labeled "mentally ill" in fact demonstrated a valid

11

Figure 2. Treating the whole is imperative in family therapy. Placing "Band-aids" on symptoms only leaves the rest of the family confused and in pain.

adaptation to the interactional patterns most prevalent in their families of origin.

Leaders in the field of family therapy such as Virginia Satir, Jay Haley, Don Jackson, and Paul Watzlawick were influenced by Bateson's study. Nathan Ackerman and Murray Bowen, psychiatrists with the Menninger Clinic, went to New York and Washington, thereby providing a major influence in family therapy on the East Coast. In the South, Carl Whitaker's research and work in family treatment had a significant influence on the future of family therapy as a professional discipline. Family research and treatment activities in Philadelphia ultimately established that city as one of the major centers of family therapy training.

In one program, social agencies in St. Paul, Minnesota, joined forces to find a more effective way to help 150 multiproblem families, families that various agencies had tried with little success to help for an average of more than 15 years. The "conjoint" approach, which became the workers' primary therapy methodology, allowed them to treat each family as a "whole" unit, exploring problems with all family members present. Approximately two-thirds of the families involved showed positive changes in their functioning, thus strongly supporting the conjoint family therapy approach.

The family therapy movement flourished during the 1960s because of the effectiveness demonstrated by these early projects and programs. At the grass-roots level, individual practitioners with a variety of professional and nonprofessional backgrounds and training performed conjoint family therapy successfully. Family therapists began to meet to discuss their methods. Books and articles on the subject began to appear. Workshops and family therapy training institutes were established, and professional graduate schools began to introduce courses in family therapy. The culmination of this growing interest was the first graduate degree in family therapy, offered in 1977 by the Hahnemann Medical College in Philadelphia.

Although systematic research documenting the positive accomplishments of family therapy is largely lacking, a number of projects around the country demonstrate its effectiveness.

The Family Treatment Unit of the Colorado Psychiatric Hospital in Denver offered a brief-term family treatment program, which allowed an entering patient along with his immediate family to be seen within 24 hours of admission. Additional family sessions were held during the hospitalization. Comparing treatment outcomes of 150 patients who went through this program with 150 patients who did not, it was found that patients in the Family Treatment Unit spent one-third as much time in the hospital as patients not in the program. A comparable reduction in cost of treatment and time lost from work was also noted.

Beier and Robinson of the University of Utah went into a rural California community that had no resident mental health services. Over a period of seven weeks, a number of adults and high school students, many with little or no previous counseling background or experience, were successfully trained to deal with family problems in the community using conjoint family interviewing as a primary technique. Seven families received counseling, three of which were considering hospitalization of a member at the outset because of that person's severe emotional problems. At the conclusion of the project, virtually all of the participating families had shown measurable improvement.

In 1970, Sacramento County, California, established a diversion project in its juvenile probation program to deal with runaways and their families. Over a two-year period, juvenile probation officers in the county received special training in family therapy techniques from Alan and Eva Leveton of the San Francisco Family Therapy Institute. As a result of the project, court petitions filed on juveniles were reduced by 80 percent, overnight detentions were reduced by 50 percent, recidivism was reduced by 25 percent, and the cost of processing the typical juvenile complaint was cut in half.

The New York State Legislature in 1973 authorized an expenditure of funds to find more effective ways of keeping children out of foster care. Nearly 1000 children and their families participated in this project. Two-thirds of the families involved were single-parent families; two-thirds of the children were anticipating placement in a foster home and the remaining one-third were already in foster care. Using a "more intensive services" approach, with the primary emphasis on helping the entire family, it was found that after six months, 92 percent of the children in the project originally anticipating foster placement were still in their own homes and 62 percent of the children who had been in foster care at the outset of the project had been able to return to their own homes. The State saved an estimated $286,000 on foster care in one year as a direct result of the project.

A recent survey conducted by Gurman and Kniskern (1978) summarized the findings of 75 studies involving 3000 cases in which improvement rates of nonbehavioral marital and family therapy approaches were examined. In cases where marital problems were treated by seeing the individual partners separately, the improvement rate was 48 percent compared to a 70 percent improvement rate for couples seen conjointly. When conjoint family therapy was used, a 75 percent improvement rate was reported. Deterioration rates were reported in 48 percent of the cases studied: 11.6 percent with individual treatment, as opposed to 5.5 percent with conjoint therapy.

Projects such as these, coupled with the authors' own experiences as practitioners and those of our colleagues, have convinced us that meeting with all family members at the same time and focusing our attention on the interactional patterns they demonstrate is one of the most effective techniques currently available for dealing with troubled families. There have been many changes in the field of family therapy since the pioneers of the 1950s labored to formulate their ideas. Today, different "schools" of family therapy are springing up around the world, each with its special area of emphasis, such as the parents' family of origin, family hierarchy, family boundaries, paradoxical directives, triangulation, and family tasks. Some schools advocate working with only the parents or perhaps one individual in the family, although all of them claim a family orientation. The authors of this book subscribe to no particular school of family therapy, although they recognize and borrow from the rich contributions to the field made by many of these theorists.

3
KEY AREAS OF FAMILY INTERACTION

What a task the family therapist faces!

Frustrated parents, after many calls and visits to the school, plead anxiously for the therapist to "make magic" and instantly correct their child's academic and behavior problems. Other parents throw up their hands in despair when their teenagers "won't listen to anything I say." Then there are the desperate pleas for help from sobbing parents who suspect their children are using drugs. The therapist also listens to children as they complain about parents who "don't understand me," or "are too strict . . . they don't trust my friends or anything I do."

The therapist knows a husband and wife who complain about a myriad of problems in their marriage — intolerable spending habits, unsatisfactory or nonexistent sexual relations, infidelity, unbearable in-laws, and destructive habits such as excessive drinking, gambling, or chronic absenteeism. At another time the therapist sees a husband and wife, submerged in the depths of their pain, who are unable to provide leadership to their children or to stimulate a trusting, growth-producing environment where caring and loving messages are openly given and received.

The therapist has watched and is aware of these clashes and discordant patterns that manifest themselves like imperfect kaleidoscopic designs against the backdrop of a family in pain. Traditionally, therapists have taken these complaints at face value and attempted to deal solely with issues that family members said were wrong. The family "culprit" (Fig. 3), whom other family members blamed, was seen in individual therapy and, in a variety of ways, admonished to stop misbehaving and try to do better.

Another approach has been to meet, separately or jointly, with family members in conflict, advising them to try harder, to give in, or to compromise on divisive points. At times such approaches may be useful, but not when they are used as the *primary* techniques for

Figure 3. The identified patient in family therapy is often seen as the "family culprit." Individual therapy tends to enhance the "you're to blame" role and may discourage individual acceptance of responsibility for family problems.

dealing with family difficulties. More often, they are probably doomed to failure and the battle rages on, with the "culprit" becoming further estranged from the rest of the family.

To the family therapist, the message is clear: if a family is to change a destructive relationship, attention must focus on what family members do and say *to* one another, not exclusively on what they say *about* each other. If efforts are concentrated on "what is said" as opposed to "how it is said," interactional patterns between family members will reveal important new information that would otherwise remain hidden.

The family in which parents complain about children who don't listen and in which children respond that parents don't understand them may suffer more from an inability to communicate satisfactorily than from what family members may initially describe as a lack of consideration or dislike toward them on the part of other family members. A family member who turns to drugs, drink, or infidelity may not be morally deficient as much as feeling unloved, unwanted, or unable to please other members with whom he or she wants to be closest. Marriage partners who fight constantly or who find it impossible to agree on how to spend their money, use their recreational time, or parent their children may suffer less from recalcitrance or unreasonableness than they do from a lack of knowledge of how to constructively define and deal with the inevitable differences that arise in every family. The child who has problems in school may not be lazy, bad, or defiant; rather, such a youngster may be reacting in confusion and frustration to the family's unrealistic and unattainable expectations. Finally, a family whose members care about each other but who cannot develop a shared interactional plan that allows for the healthy development of its members may be trapped under a set of paralyzing interactional rules that are ineffective, difficult to change, and painful.

A number of variables affect a family's healthy or unhealthy functioning. As indicated earlier, the authors view these variables from a process standpoint, which allows them to view all behaviors — all interactional patterns — as dynamic and alive and as having some degree of interrelationship and interdependence. It is important to be aware of the "cause and effect" relationship — the "connectedness" — between all human activity and the healthy growth of an individual as well as a family system. This process orientation is essential to the following discussion of the key areas of family interactional patterns that are found in family systems.

Although there are too many possible areas of family interaction to consider all of them, the following pages do reflect all family systems — functional or dysfunctional — and present the key interactional patterns that the authors have seen occur and recur in both functional nurturing families and dysfunctional troubled families. Of course, the patterns differ in functional families and dysfunctional families. For example, healthy, growth-producing families tend to communicate in a clear and direct manner, while dysfunctional families often transmit messages in a vague and indirect manner. Table 1 illustrates some of the contrasts in functional and dysfunctional families' interactional patterns. Families rarely fall at extreme ends on the continuum. Rather, they tend to be dynamic and fluctuate from one point to another within the different areas.

As most therapists are aware, the distinction between functional and dysfunctional interactional patterns is seldom as extreme or clear as depicted in the table. The therapist should objectively decide whether a family's interactional patterns are functional or dysfunctional based on their healthy or unhealthy use in the family system.

Families are not always able to develop and maintain positive patterns of interaction (see Fig. 4); at times, these patterns become confusing and pain-producing to family members. It is important to emphasize that, though the authors focus on the breakdowns in family interactions, they do not imply that the interactional areas themselves are negative. They do, however, hope to amplify the importance of each area and demonstrate the impact that unsuccessful resolution of breakdowns have on the family system.

The discussion of breakdowns is limited to those interactional areas previously discussed, but even within these limits, the discussion of breakdowns is far from complete because of the uniqueness of all family systems. Moreover, distinctions between these interac-

Table 1. Continuum of Dysfunctional and Functional Family Patterns

Criteria	Dysfunctional	Functional
Family climate	Blaming, painful, distrusting	Trusting, growth-producing, "feeling good" atmosphere
Key family interactional patterns	Unique dysfunctional patterns	Healthy functional patterns
Communication	Indirect, controlled, vague	Verbally and nonverbally direct and clear
Self-concept reinforcement	Unsupportive, low self-esteem, blaming	Supportive, high self-esteem, loving
Members' expectations	Judgmental, rigid, controlling	Flexible, realistic, individualized
Handling of differences	Attacking, avoiding, surrendering	Tolerant, dynamic, negotiating
Family rules	Contradictory, self-defeating, rigid	Workable, constructive, flexible

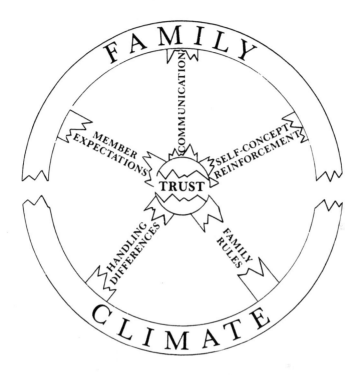

Figure 4. When breakdowns in interactional patterns occur, the resulting shock can splinter the entire family system.

tional breakdowns become vague as they frequently touch and overlap. For example, a family that has difficulty giving its members adequate self-concept reinforcement may not have learned adequate communication techniques. Another family may be locked into unsatisfying relationships because of the mutually held expectation that all members must agree on everything; such families believe that it is destructive to show disagreement. The *unique* ways in which members of particular families communicate, show love, and deal with differences may actually cause problems in other areas of their relationships. Before a family can be helped to deal effectively with its problems, both the therapist and the family members must have a basic awareness of the primary interactional patterns occurring within the group. The family therapist plans and implements interventions around these process-area breakdowns.

As the pain-producing interactions through which a family has been mishandling situations become more apparent to its members, individuals previously labeled as being insensitive, uncaring, or vindictive will be seen in a new dimension. The family will begin to experience a feeling of hopefulness rather than discouragement and despair.

The belief that "tomorrow can be better" is one of the keystones of growth, "the light at the end of the tunnel" that all of us need.

Communication

Even in its most basic form, the seemingly simple, yet infinitely complex process of one person transmitting information to another contains innumerable possibilities for breakdowns in family relationships. Loderer and Jackson (1968) point out that even in the closest family relationships spouses probably miscommunicate 20 percent of the time because of such factors as cultural differences, unique maturation experiences, and differing perceptions.

The following is a description of a few of the more frequent breakdowns the authors have observed.

Expressing Feelings / Family members do not clearly discuss their feelings with each other. Frequently a discrepancy is noted between the *words* a person says and the nonverbal aspects of the message, such as tone, posture, and facial expression. The person sending a message may feel fearful or uncomfortable with what he anticipates the receiver's response will be. As a result, his words will not reflect his true feelings and the spoken and experienced message is not the same for either person. Frequently, parents who grew up in a family where this ineffective type of communication pattern persisted never learned to be open in expressing their feelings and are unable to model open expression of feelings for their children.

> Bob was offered a position with an oil company that would double his salary but would keep him away from home up to three weeks every month. He mentioned the offer at the dinner table one evening, but failed to ask specifi-

cally what each family member thought about the job, because he was afraid no one would really care what he did. His wife didn't like the prospect of his prolonged absences but commented only that the family could use the extra money. A teenage son said nothing, thinking his dad would take the job to get away from conflicts at home, although he actually didn't want his father to be away from home so much. Bob took the new job, but felt hurt because the extra income seemed more important to the family than his presence in the home.

Indirect Communication / Family members communicate indirectly, frequently through a third member of the family. This position of family mediator is most often assumed by mothers. The family mediator typically experiences feelings of both burden and power in this role. She generally perceives herself to be the family peacemaker and makes her services available to family members who fear direct contact with another family member because of the rejection and negative response they believe they will get from that member.

> Dad is very upset with Linda, his teenage daughter, because she has been keeping late hours. He doesn't want Linda to be angry with him and dreads dealing with Linda's tears and possible temper tantrum if he talks directly to her. He shares his discomfort with his wife, hoping she will make their daughter aware of his grievances.

Failure to Listen / Family members fail to listen to what other family members try to tell them and therefore miss the message. Human beings, unless they are hearing disabled, usually *hear* what they are told, but they do not always listen. Generally, failing to listen is an unproductive defense mechanism resulting from unresolved anger, preoccupation, or a deliberate effort to tune out what is perceived or expected to be painful information. Although simplistic, this unproductive pattern is a major contributor to family dysfunction.

> Lori is 17 and involved in many school activities. She usually rides to and from school with her brother Bill, who works nearby. He doesn't get off work until an hour after Lori is finished at school. Lori, wanting to earn some ex-

tra money to buy a car of her own, approaches her mother about taking a part-time job at a local drive-in restaurant. Her mother is certain Lori simply wants an excuse to meet boys and run around with them after work. She becomes furious and says, "No daughter of mine will ever work at a place like that! You don't need a car anyway. All you would do if you had one is run around, pick up boys, and go to parties." Discouraged, Lori quickly realizes that, once again, what she said and what her mother heard were poles apart.

Faulty Assumptions / Family members make assumptions about what other members know, think, or feel and act as though these assumptions were fact (see Fig. 5). Popularly referred to as "mind-reading," this communication breakdown most often takes one of the following two forms:

1. A family member expects other members to know what he or she wants or needs. Without expressing these wants or needs, the family member anticipates that other members will magically discern and automatically act on fulfilling them.

Elaine becomes upset upon returning from a meeting, because her husband did not make their teenage son do the dinner dishes left in the sink. Before leaving, however, Elaine had told neither her husband nor their son that she wanted the dishes done.

2. A family member assumes he knows what other members want or are feeling without checking with other members to determine whether his assumptions are accurate.

Harry volunteers the services of his two teenage sons to help clean out an elderly neighbor's garage on Saturday but doesn't check first on the boys' plans for the weekend. The boys had planned to go to the lake with friends on Saturday. They are irate with their father. A family fight ensues, and as a result, the boys are grounded for a week.

Monitoring or Controlling of Behavior / Family members try to monitor and control the communications of other family members.

Figure 5.   When family members make assumptions about what other members know, think, or feel (mind reading), they often conjure up fantasies that are distorted.

Monitoring frequently emerges as the result of messages from other members expressing anger, disagreement, pain, or other feelings with which the "controlling member" is uncomfortable. The member doing the silencing is often a parent, while the member being silenced is frequently a child. Gerald Zuk (1971) has labeled such maneuvers "silencing strategies," a major purpose of which is to keep family skeletons locked in the closet (see Fig. 6). Silencing strategies emerge in many ways and may include a family member changing the subject, ignoring a question of another member, or suddenly laughing or coughing as well as other nonverbal ploys. Strategies such as these signal the speaker to stop what he is saying or doing or to change to a less painful and dangerous subject.

Figure 6. Family members often try to monitor and control the communication of other family members. The purpose of these "silencing strategies" is often to keep family skeletons locked in the closet.

The therapist is meeting for the third time with Julie and her family. Julie's mother had dominated previous sessions with consistent and vivid descriptions of Julie's inappropriate behavior. Julie has listened glumly and only occasionally has glanced at her mother. Each glance reflects the girl's anger and resentment at her mother's accusations. Suddenly, Julie refers to her mother's drinking. Immediately, the mother directs a penetrating stare at her. Julie gets the message and does not pursue the subject. She lapses back into resentful silence.

Double-bind Messages / Family members send impossible-response messages to other members. Commonly referred to in family therapy literature as "double-bind" messages, the receiver always experiences a "damned if I do and damned if I don't" feeling and a "no-win" outcome.

> Pete's dad has been nagging him to get out and mix more with other kids. One of Pete's teachers coaches a Little League baseball team. The boy decides to join the team, with the encouragement of the teacher. The team plays its games after school on Mondays. Pete excitedly informs his dad of his decision. The father responds by saying: "You can't do that! You know Monday is my day off and I expect you to help me with the yard work when you get home from school!"

Self-concept Reinforcement

The manner in which children see and value themselves is influenced most significantly by the messages they receive concerning their value to other members of the family. Messages that convey praise, approval, appreciation, trust, and confidence in decisions and that allow family members to pursue individual needs and ultimately to become independent are the foundation blocks of a child's feelings of self-worth. Adults also need and depend heavily on this kind of reinforcement for their own emotional well-being.

Families that have difficulty reinforcing and strengthening each member's self-concept find that the thread binding members together into perfect kaleidoscopic patterns of support is thereby weakened. As a result, family members feel unloved or unwanted and grasp for a sign of being worth something to others.

Following are examples of common breakdowns in a family's support system.

Denigrating Messages / Family members feel unloved by other members and receive messages of being "not much good." They do not receive reinforcing or supporting messages concerning their self-worth from other members. Sometimes messages are blocked out or negated by a person's storehouse of preexisting bad feelings about himself.

> Larry, in an institution for delinquent boys, tells his therapist not to bother checking with his parents to see whether he can go home for Christmas. He is certain they will enjoy the holidays much more if he isn't there.

Lack of Supportive Messages / Family members fail to send reinforcing and supportive messages to other family members for many reasons. Often, they don't know how.

> "Kids are too soft these days. My wife says I don't praise our kids enough. My old man didn't praise us but he sure let us know when we were doing something wrong. I don't think any of us turned out too bad."

In other cases family members aren't around to give the needed reinforcement of self-esteem because they have chosen instead to devote their time to work, community, recreational, or professional activities, or other people such as friends or extended family members. A relationship that is not nurtured by an adequate investment of time and energy on the part of its members will eventually wither and die.

> "Dad works as a salesman in a men's clothing store during the week. He doesn't eat with the family very often but usually grabs a sandwich downtown before going to his second job at the liquor store. He's around on Sundays but Mom is at church more than half the day. If us kids don't go to church and Sunday school with Mom, we sleep late and then take off with our friends for the rest of the day."

Another reason that family members don't build each other's self-esteem is that their own needs are not being met and they don't feel good about themselves. As a result, their own ability to offer sensitivity, empathy, and caring is significantly lowered, and their interactions with other family members inevitably become destructive to everyone's self-worth. Blame, accusations, ridicule, and tense, uneasy silences permeate interactional dynamics.

> "I guess I'm aware that the rest of the family sees me as a nag and a crab. It's hard to do much else, particularly when the main reason people seem to want me around is to pick up after them, cook their meals, keep the house clean, and ask as little of them as possible. They never volunteer to help with anything. Praise for an especially good meal is virtually unheard of but just let me fix something they don't like . . ."

Failure to Receive Messages / Family members may have different modes and styles of sending caring messages to each other. These styles may have been influenced by a parent's family of origin or by unique life experiences combined with their special personalities and temperaments. A relationship problem arises when one family member believes that in order to be genuine, caring can be shown only through ways that are familiar to, acceptable to, and demonstrated by him. This person may fail to recognize that there are different ways of sending caring messages and may perceive an unfamiliar mode of expression as a threat. In effect he is saying: "If you don't love and accept me in the ways I show you love and acceptance, it must mean you just don't care."

> Mother's family openly and physically demonstrated love and caring. Dad's family tended to be quiet, reserved, and uncomfortable with physical displays of affection. It is becoming increasingly difficult for Mother to live without these frequent and effusive displays of physical affection. Dad prefers the company of his family to other people and is usually home, but Mother has a growing doubt about his love for her and believes he takes her too much for granted. Bringing the subject up with him seems only to cause him to be defensive and even more withdrawn. Two of her husband's most frequent responses are "I don't know what you want," and "It seems that anything I do is wrong."

Taking Over / A family member fails to permit another member to develop a sense of responsibility and self-worth through successful management of his own life. This most often occurs when one member is told consistently how to do things or when a member steps in and carries out responsibilities that should have been performed by another member. Such a state of affairs is frequently found in parent–child relationships and may go so far as to involve more than two generations, although husband–wife relationships are not immune from this pattern.

> Sandy was divorced two years ago and her mother, Beatrice, moved in to help with the children. Beatrice constantly corrects Sandy and makes most of the decisions concerning the children. Sandy resents her mother's domination but is too unsure of her own parenting skills to confront Beatrice. Her frustration is expressed by her youngest son, who says, "Gee, Mama, Grandma tells you what to do just like she does us."

> When Eric has behavior problems at school, his father always arranges to take time off from work to meet with the vice-principal or anyone else who is available. Frequently, he does not agree with the way the school handles the situation and never hesitates to share his dissatisfaction with his son and the school's authorities.

Family Members' Expectations

Consciously or unconsciously, every human being has some expectations concerning the outcome of any life situation they experience. Family living is no exception.

The expectations a newly married couple brings to the relationship are influenced significantly by earlier experiences. Both partners continue to invest in their past by attempting to carry on many patterns from their families of origin or, if their earlier family experiences were consciously disappointing, by rejecting them. Each partner in a new marriage has faced unique earlier experiences and each possesses a unique personality, so the expectations each brings to a new family will not be the same. Some accommodation of the differences will be necessary for peaceful and productive coexistence. Familial expectations that are stubbornly clung to often are transferred to children by one or both parents, particularly in terms of how children should behave, what they should achieve, how they should spend their time, with whom they should associate, and how they should express themselves. Fulfillment of these expectations by their children may be especially compelling for parents who find their purpose for being and the primary validation of their own self-worth in the actions of their children. Such parents see their children as being an extension of themselves and frequently have expectations that the child will be able to do and be all that they have dreamed of doing and becoming but have not accomplished. They may also see in a failure by their child a message to the whole world that they have failed as parents. Problems caused by expectations of family members that the therapist should be most concerned about include the following:

Ignoring Individuality / Family members may expect others to do things or behave in ways that do not fit with the latters' individuality or current life situation. Frequently, these expectations come from memories of how a parent's family of origin or a family he admired did things. Sometimes these expectations come from idealistic thinking concerning family behavior and management. For example, a parent might want other family members to invest their time, energy, and money in activities that are of little interest to them or may expect them to behave in a prescribed manner that does not fit their behavioral style, interest, or inclinations.

> Greg's father and grandfather hold comfortable, well-paying office jobs with a local company. Everyone in the family, particularly Dad and Grandpa, think Greg will go to work for the company when he graduates from college. But Greg has the talent and interest to be a good artist. His father labels Greg's ambition a complete waste of time and brands art as an "unmanly occupation." Greg's future is no longer discussed at home because of the bitter battles it provokes with his father. Dad is further irritated by Greg's failing grades in the business courses the boy has been forced to take in high school.

Proving Love / Family members place expectations on others' behavior that are used as standards by which the "expecting member" determines how much the other members care for him. The message attached to these expectations is: "If you will not be as I wish you to be, you don't love me."

> Grace believes weekends should be reserved primarily for the family to do things together around the house. Her husband insists that he works hard during the week and should be able to use his weekends to relax, play golf, go hunting, or enjoy football. He has asked Grace to join him but she steadfastly refuses, feeling that he is selfish and is not sensitive to her wishes. If he did care, she reasons, he would want to please her by working on the house and garage.

Handling Differences

A faulty yet relatively well-entrenched expectation in many families is the idea that family members should see eye-to-eye on most things and should agree with each other most of the time.

Clichés such as "two become as one" do little to prepare couples for the inevitable differences of both perception and opinion that must accompany any marriage. Serious problems in a family's functioning appear when differences become equated with "badness" or when disagreement is seen as "not caring."

Family members have four basic techniques with which to deal with differences that arise between them. The first three techniques rarely lead to a successful resolution of differences while the fourth is frequently effective in doing so.

Attack / One family member lashes out at another member. A difference of opinion often deteriorates into a direct personal attack and may be manifested by blaming another person, bringing up the past, making destructive comparisons, or lashing out with other expressions of anger and hurt.

> Mother frequently becomes sarcastic and accuses other family members of being inconsiderate when they do not

behave as she thinks they should or express opinions and ideas different from her own.

Avoidance / Disagreements are not acknowledged or discussed openly, often because individuals lack the skills to carry on a constructive discussion. A family member who avoids might say: "I'm afraid I'll lose my temper if I try to discuss our differences," or "I never could express myself, especially when I get upset." Such a person avoids discussions of differences, fearing that the person with whom he disagrees will withdraw approval or become angry when learning of the disagreement. It is impossible to settle a problem without first acknowledging its presence.

> Dad works hard and can't understand why he can't have a little peace and quiet when he comes home at night. Arguments between his wife and their 16-year-old daughter are becoming louder and more frequent with each of them expecting him to take her side. Dad wants no part of their battles and lately has been finding reasons to return to the shop after supper.

Surrender / A difference of opinion or disagreement may be acknowledged, but at least one person either avoids expressing personal needs or wishes or does so in a superficial way. Ultimately, this person goes along with others, often at the price of denying his or her own needs. Again, this position is generally taken to avoid angering another family member or losing approval and support.

> Connie learned long ago not to argue with her mother and older sister, particularly when they are in agreement. She has known Bob for a long time and likes him, but her mother and sister disapprove of the relationship and insist that she stop seeing him. Connie, trying to avoid angry confrontations, has tried to see Bob during the day at school but her family has learned of these meetings. Connie has decided that it is easier to stop seeing Bob than to face daily fights with her family.

Negotiation / This complex but ultimately workable procedure for dealing with differences involves an open, nonattacking expression of one's position, a willingness to hear, respect, and search for merit in the positions of other people involved, and an ability to identify basic areas of agreement. Individuals involved in successful negotiation are able to modify their own expectations without denying their needs. This leads to a workable solution with which everyone can live. An example of a family successfully utilizing negotiation to deal with the different priorities of its members follows:

> Roger's report card was a shock to his parents and, to a lesser degree, to him. He failed one subject and barely passed two others. Roger knew his disappointing grades were due to spending too much time on a part-time job, but he was unwilling to give it up. The problem was compounded by the fact that when he left the job around 7:30 P.M., he didn't feel like going home to study. Roger and his parents sat down to discuss the problem. They agreed that Roger would keep his job but would work longer on Saturday and shorter hours after school. Roger decided that some of the things he wants to buy with the additional income he can earn by working long hours will have to wait awhile and that getting better grades in school was more important.

Unique Dysfunctional Interactional Patterns

All families develop a number of recurring, predictable interactional patterns, frequently labeled "family rules." These patterns usually operate at more than one level of a family's awareness and provide the security for family members that comes from predictability. These patterns may be used to communicate with each other, give self-concept reinforcement, formulate and express expectations, and handle differences — all interactional areas discussed previously. They then, in essence, become a kaleidoscopic code that guides individual family members into predictable and recurrent patterns of design.

Luthman and Kirschenbaum (1974) suggest, in *The Dynamic Family*, that if a particular interactional pattern occurs more than three times in a family session, a family rule probably exists. Sometimes these rules are workable and constructive, but often they become contradictory, self-defeating, and destructive because they are born out of, and perpetuated by, fear of change or reprisal or a lack of knowledge as to how a given situation might be handled differently. Furthermore, because the existence of specific family rules is frequently outside a family's conscious awareness, the rules are not subject to discussion and arbitration. At times, the existence of identified family rules may be vehemently denied.

Family therapists are especially concerned with the following repetitive, interactional patterns.

PATTERNS THAT CAUSE PEOPLE PAIN

Rule / "Never admit you're wrong."

> No one in the Brown family ever apologizes or admits they made a mistake. Family members are cool to each other for a day or two when feelings are hurt, but they never directly tell anyone why they are upset or say they are sorry.

Rule / "We have always done it this way and we always will."

> The Smith family drives to a neighboring town every Sunday to spend the day with Mrs. Smith's mother. Secretly, family members often would rather do something else. The visits frequently are unpleasant since the grandmother is openly critical of the fact that Mrs. Smith works and is convinced that the job is the cause of her grandchildren's misbehavior. "After all," she states repeatedly, "their mother isn't around to raise them properly."

PATTERNS THAT PERPETUATE OR INTENSIFY PROBLEMS RATHER THAN SOLVE THEM

Rule / "Don't talk about unpleasant things."

> The Harris children have been instructed by their mother not to bother their father with unpleasant things when he comes home from work because he is tired. Since so many topics are potentially unpleasant, the children have learned

that it is safer to say as little as possible to their father. Ideas they have and actions they are contemplating are never checked out in advance with their father. He frequently is unhappy with his children's behavior and wonders why they do things he considers improper.

Rule / "Blame someone else."

The Lewis family agrees that Jeff has always been a difficult child. When something goes wrong, the boy generally is involved. Jeff has come to believe he can do nothing right and has all but given up trying to get along with other family members and to do things that please them. The boy's parents reject the idea of family therapy because "Jeff is the problem."

PATTERNS THAT ARE IN CONFLICT WITH EACH OTHER

Rule / "Evening meals are important times of family togetherness."

Subrule / "When the family gets together, Dad can tell the others what he doesn't like about them."

Dad insists that all members of the family eat dinner together every evening. No one may leave the table until everyone is finished because dinnertime is one of the few times left when the family can be together. Yet Dad frequently uses the time to reprimand Bobby about his poor grades in math, to scold Ann for her sloppy room, or to make not-so-subtle gibes at Mother for "spending all day on the telephone and never getting anything accomplished."

Rule / "Behave yourself and achieve in school."

Subrule / "It's understandable if you don't respect your teachers."

Mr. and Mrs. Martin are furious with their son Billy when they are called to the principal's office after Billy has been suspended from school for swearing and talking back to his English teacher. He is soundly spanked and all his privileges are removed for the next month. Yet comments such as "If you fail at everything else, you can always teach," or "When common sense was handed out, teachers must have been out to lunch," frequently are made by both parents.

FAMILY VALUES

As the therapist moves to identify dysfunctional family interactional patterns, he or she must also be sensitive to a family's value system (the things they believe to be important in life). Family values can significantly influence the establishment of family rules such as "work before play" and "academic achievement is all-important." Family rules, clung to tenaciously over a period of time, can sometimes harden into family values.

Family values are frequently indicated by how a family spends its time and money. Family values can be vital in determining the kinds of goals a family is willing to set for itself in therapy and how hard members are willing to work to reach those goals. Growth-producing values are generally characterized by openness, respect, honesty, and caring, while destructive family values are usually spawned by personal insecurity and carry attributes such as greed, power, dishonesty, and disregard for others. Destructive family values can change as a family experiences, both in therapy and in living, the rewards of openly sharing feelings, acknowledging and appreciating the uniqueness of individual members, trusting people, and valuing themselves and their needs.

Origins of a family's dysfunctional interactional patterns are frequently obscure, but many come from parents' own growing-up experiences. Dysfunctional interactional patterns often are outside the conscious awareness of family members. There is disagreement among family therapists as to whether or not these patterns must be brought to a family's conscious awareness before they can be influenced by the therapeutic process, particularly when the purpose of the patterns is to avoid pain and/or retain control.

Family Climate

"What it feels like to be a member of this family" is an outcome of the interplay of the family interactions discussed earlier. Feelings are a human being's gut-level reaction to experience. Feelings operate at different levels of intensity and consciousness.

We reach inside to grasp our feelings, which are generally the conscious or unconscious foundation of our perception of the world. Feelings are real, and though they may be consciously denied, they cannot be dismissed.

Every interaction that a family member experiences with a spouse, parent, or child produces certain reactions or feelings within that member. Sometimes these feelings are unique to each member; more frequently, they are shared. The blend produced from family members' nonverbal and verbal sharing and interacting might be called "family climate."

A family therapist soon becomes proficient at gauging a family's climate as he or she shares time and space with the family. Constructive family interactional patterns are reflected in openness, appropriate humor and laughter, expressions of caring, mutual respect, a valuing of the quality of each individual, and a general feeling of well-being. Dysfunctional interactional patterns manifest themselves in tension, pain, many kinds of physical disability, frustration, guilt, persistent anger, and a feeling of hopelessness.

Tension, apprehension, and a feeling of heaviness pervaded the room (Fig. 7). Glenn and Beth Hanson sat rigidly on the couch, as far apart as possible. Neither Glenn nor Beth glanced at each other during the session. Glenn's legs were crossed and his right foot frequently bobbed up and down, adding to the tension of the session. The oldest son, Brent, obviously wishing he could leave, leaned against the door frame leading into the kitchen. Several times he abruptly left the living room, supposedly to get something to eat or drink. Connie, sitting across from her parents, thumbed through a magazine lying on the coffee table and responded to questions or comments from the therapist or other family members with a surprised look and the question, "What did you say?"

Trust

As schematized in Figure 8, trust is the hub of all family interactions, the connecting link among family members. When a therapist first begins to observe and experience a family's interactional patterns, a climate of trust or mistrust will quickly emerge.

It was the first session with the Johnson family. With the exception of Mom, the family members reflected the usual anxiety and apprehension that is present in families beginning a new experience. Mom was eager to get started. She began expressing her concerns even before everyone was seated. After some rules for sharing information were established, all the family members began to express themselves freely. Although the family was experiencing considerable pain, they seemed to be open and willing to listen and share with each other. The climate was tense but hopeful. Controlling and manipulative behaviors

Figure 7. A family therapist soon becomes proficient at gauging a family's climate. The tension and apprehension between Glenn and Beth Hanson were apparent as they sat rigidly on the couch, as far apart as possible.

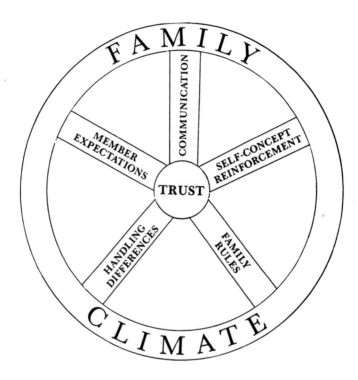

Figure 8. Family interactional patterns can be viewed like a wheel. At the hub of the wheel is trust, and the interactional patterns operate through the stability or instability of its center. Like the wheel, the "family climate" is the rim or the outer shell of the family.

were at a minimum. Although the atmosphere became very strained when discussing the son's drug use, the family was able to express hoped-for outcomes.

The issue of trust must be dealt with in the beginning sessions. If some degree of minimal trust is not established during early sessions, future sessions will be destined for failure.

This was the second session with the Jackson family. They had been referred to therapy by the Municipal Court after the son, Mel (16), was arrested for shoplifting. The shoplifting incident had actually occurred 30 days prior to the first family session. It was the first incident Mel had been involved in, and since the incident, his behavior had been exemplary. Mr. Jackson had placed very tight restrictions on Mel since the incident, which included no outside school activities, no use of the phone or car, and television only on weekends. Mr. Jackson insisted these restrictions were necessary to "teach Mel a lesson," and they allowed him to know what Mel was doing at all times. When confronted with the exemplary behavior on Mel's part, both prior to and since the incident, Mr. Jackson replied that he felt his son was probably involved in a lot of things he knew nothing about and was fooling everyone. He then indicated that he "wouldn't be fooled again."

The therapist must deal with the issue of trust on two levels: On one level, the therapist should be sensitive to the degree of trust that exists among individual family members and the overall climate or atmosphere of the family. On a second level, the therapist must be aware of the degree of trust or distrust that exists between him and the individual family members and the family as a whole.

An awareness on both these levels of trust will directly affect the type and timing of interventions utilized by the therapist. In Chapter 4, the authors discuss various approaches to beginning family sessions. The suggested approaches in Chapter 4 and in Chapter 6 will provide the reader with suggestions on establishing and evaluating trust on both levels.

Becoming Aware of Interactional Patterns

Changing the focus of therapy from the client's definition of the problem to what family members are doing to each other is not a simple task, nor does it happen immediately. The beginning family therapist must spend some time becoming attuned to the interactional areas described previously before attempting to help a family deal with its problems.

The following suggestions describe a few ways the therapist might become familiar with key family interactions. One of the most helpful ways for the neophyte therapist to tune in to the family process is to observe and/or listen to a number of family therapy interviews. Sources for such interviews include:

1.   Filmed or videotaped family interviews by skilled family therapists. One of the best sets of family therapy training films available to help sensitize beginning therapists to family processes are the five films produced by Alan and Eva Leveton of the San Francisco Family Therapy Institute. Especially relevant are the two films, *Family Process* and *Family Rules*, plus the *Candy* interview. Information on other available family therapy films may be obtained from sources such as those listed in the Appendices.

2.   Audiotapes or videotapes of family interviews done by other family therapists or even a beginning session with a family that the therapist has done himself. Because there is often no one else with family counseling skills available in the community, therapists in rural states have to meet with a family before they possess adequate family therapy skills. In such a setting the therapist may have no choice but to dive in and begin working with a family. By critically listening to or viewing a tape of the session (possibly with a colleague or supervisor and always with a family's consent), a therapist often can identify more objectively the interplay between family members.

3.   Observing live family interviews conducted by other therapists. The observation may include viewing a session through a one-way mirror or sitting in on the interview and assuming the role of co-therapist. Sharing perceptions after a session with the primary therapist and receiving feedback will provide the beginning therapist with an invaluable learning experience.

4.   Role-playing a simulated family with other therapists, noting the interactional processes that occur. It is frequently helpful in beginning simulated family interviews to structure a situation and give "family members" some guidelines for their roles, especially with people who have done very little role-playing. The simulated family interview frequently depicts an initial session, with one or two participants taking the role of family therapists. The simulated family may be patterned after a real family with which one of the role players is familiar. In such situations the person presenting the

family should assume the role of a key family member. New therapists should concentrate initially on observing and identifying one or two family interactional areas and, as they become more proficient, gradually increase the number of interactions on which they attempt to focus. Keeping track of the interactions occurring between several family members may seem overwhelming at first, so the new therapist might consider initially focusing attention on the interactions going on between two family members, noting how they communicate and give each other reinforcement, what they expect of each other, how they handle differences, and so on. Next, an attempt should be made to identify areas of breakdown. These guidelines should assist in identification of specific interactional patterns.

FAMILY COMMUNICATION PATTERNS

Be especially sensitive in family conversations to who is included and who is left out. Do verbal and nonverbal messages sent by family members agree? Do family members appear open and direct in expressing their concerns and feelings toward one another? Do people listen to each other? Do they seem tuned in to each other's needs? Are messages frequently misunderstood? Is there a family "mediator"? Do people check out the meaning of a message when it is not clear? Are mind-reading, silencing of other members, or "impossible response" messages present in the family communications?

Virgina Satir (1975, 1976), in *Changing with Families* and *Helping Families to Change,* identifies helpful exercises for emphasizing and experiencing key family communication stances. Using Satir's exercises, therapists can role-play with simulated families, providing each "family member" with a card describing one of these stances and then asking each of them to deal with a particular family situation communicating from the assigned role. Observers then are asked to identify the communication stance of each person.

Satir cites four problematic communication stances, each possessing infinite variations and combinations:

1. Placating: Appeasing, reconciling differences, handling with kid gloves, gently covering up. "Let's bury the hatchet and make up."

2. Distracting: Steering clear of disagreements, shying away from problems, giving in to others, pretending not to understand, changing the subject. "I don't want to get involved." "Don't rock the boat."

3. Blaming: Criticizing, judging, controlling, comparing. "Why can't you be like your sister?" "It's all your fault."

4. Being super reasonable: Being calm, controlled, detached, beyond reproach, giving intellectual responses. "In my opinion . . ." "It appears . . ."

SELF-CONCEPT REINFORCEMENT

Development of a chart when observing or listening to a family interview is helpful in keeping track of the number of positive and negative verbal messages that each member sends to others. The family therapist should also give attention to silent messages occurring between family members rather than relying strictly on verbal messages. Look for tender glances and comforting touches that family members might use to confirm feeling for one another. A completed chart can offer valuable information on the frequency with which caring messages are expressed, who sends them, who receives them, who gets left out, and the amount of contact and warmth that is shared between all the possible dyadic combinations in the family.

Figure 9 illustrates one family's reinforcement patterns. Ron is quickly identified as the family scapegoat since he receives largely negative messages from other family members and initiates little contact with them. Tammy is identified as the "good child." Communication between Ted, the father, and the children is limited. The more family sessions the therapist observes utilizing the chart, the more reliable an identification technique it becomes for a family's patterns of self-concept reinforcement.

MEMBER EXPECTATION IDENTIFICATION

Be sensitive to disappointments family members express about one another, particularly if the disappointments are repeated. Stated and restated disappointments indicate expectations members hold for other members that are not being met. Also, note directing re-

Senders	Receivers				
	Ted	Ginger	Kevin	Ron	Tammy
Ted (Father)	╲	+ + + - - - + - -	- - - + + -	- - - - - + -	+ + +
Ginger (Mother)	+ + + - - + - + - +	╲	+ + - - + - + - - + + +	- - + + - - + - + - -	+ + + - + + + +
Kevin	- - + -	+ + - + +		- - + - - - -	+ +
Ron	- + - 	+ + - -	- - + 		+ -
Tammy	+ + +	+ + + + + - + +	+ - + +	+ - - + -	

Figure 9. Measuring reinforcing messages sent and received by family members. As the family's interactions are observed during the interview, the therapists indicate the positive messages that one family member sends another by marking a (+) in the box shared by the sender and receiver of the message on the line parallel with the sender's name. Negative messages sent by one family member to another are marked with a (−).

quests like "do this" or "be this" that one member makes of another that are resisted or not well-received, particularly if they recur. Is an unrealistic expectation involved?

IDENTIFYING PATTERNS OF HANDLING DIFFERENCES

Note family conflicts or areas of disagreements. Try to identify patterns concerning the manner in which a family usually deals with these conflicts. Attempt to identify patterns with predictable outcomes that indicate how a family deals with conflict. Frequently, in training sessions, the authors use simulated families that are facing prescribed situations and whose members hold differing opinions as to how they should be resolved. Each family member is given a card that describes his or her stance — attack, avoid, surrender, negotiate. The manner in which the "family" handles the differences is noted and observers are asked to identify: (1) the manner in which each member deals with the difference, (2) where the breakdown in resolving differences occurred, and (3) which family members need to change their behaviors before the problem can be resolved.

IDENTIFYING A FAMILY'S UNIQUE DYSFUNCTIONAL INTERACTIONAL PATTERNS (DIPS)

Family DIPS, or rules, can be subtle and not immediately identifiable. For this reason, it frequently may be necessary to observe and/or listen to a mechanically recorded family interview more than once to recognize unique interactional patterns. Observing two or more counseling sessions with the same family can make the identification of the family DIPS more reliable. As mentioned earlier, the best clue in identifying a unique interactional pattern in a family is to determine the frequency with which it occurs. Do family members interact with each other in a particular way on several occasions during the session with every member playing his or her role in the interaction in a similar manner? If so, a family rule probably has been identified.

Another exercise suggested by Eva Leveton (1976) to sensitize beginners to family DIPS is role-playing a simulated family in which *each member* is given a specific rule that he or she is requested to follow in all interactions with other family members. Observers are asked to identify the family rules they see in operation during a discussion of a report card that the son has brought home from school. Family members are given three rules that guide their interactions with one another. Dad: "It's all Jerry's fault"; Mom: "If my husband spent more time with the family, there would be no problems"; Jerry: "Avoid hassles." Obviously, the parents display a blaming attitude in this interaction and the son has little to say. Nothing is accomplished.

FAMILY CLIMATE IDENTIFICATION

The therapist must be aware of his own inner feelings before identifying a family's climate. As he watches, listens to and experiences family sessions, he must identify his own feelings. Is he experiencing tension, tiredness, hopefulness, anger, or boredom? Some or all of the family members may be experiencing the same kinds of feelings. The therapist need not limit his efforts to tune in to his own feelings to therapy sessions. He can gain valuable practice in identifying family climate by letting his senses tell him what people in a family are feeling when he is with them in social or related situations. Provided he doesn't overdo it, he may begin looking at his own family interactions and attempt to become aware of the existing emotional climate. The value of family climate identification exercises is greatly enhanced whenever the therapist has an opportunity to check out his perceptions with the people he is with to determine whether he is on the right track.

4
BEGINNING FAMILY THERAPY

The Arndt family occupies all but two chairs in the waiting room of the juvenile therapist's office (Fig. 10). Tension and discord permeate the room like a cloud. The feelings of hurt and misunderstanding make it difficult to distinguish the kaleidoscopic array of interactional patterns that exist within the family. Bob, the father, a tall, determined man, checks his watch and wonders whether he will get back to the office in time for his next appointment. He wonders why the therapist asked him to come to this session. He has done everything possible to get his son, Ted, back on the track. Laura, the mother, glances nervously at Bob. She is aware of his discomfort and fears the therapy session will end up as just another bitter and pointless argument between Ted and her husband that leaves everyone in the family shaken. Glenda, like her father, is not sure why she had to miss her band session to see the therapist. She wasn't picked up last week for breaking a window; Ted was. She wonders whether things might be better at home if Ted went somewhere else to live. Maybe Dad was right when he told him so last night. Ted sits scrunched up in the corner, away from the family, his face buried in an old magazine. His manner projects defiance, but he is afraid and angry. Apprehension fills the room and hope is weak. But hope, though only a glimmer, is present or the family would not be here, together. How well the therapist is able to explore and build on that hope will be a major factor in determining whether the family returns for future therapy.

Figure 10.   When families are entering therapy, the natural anxiety and fear that accompany a new experience are present in each member. Apprehension may fill the room, but hope is also present.

Whom Do You See?

Families should be seen together in therapy sessions for several reasons: Developing an understanding of a family's interactional patterns or how they relate to each other depends on seeing this relationship in action with all members present. Individual family members can tell what things are like in their family, but inevitably these perceptions are flawed by their own pain and needs. As a result, the therapist has only a piece of the puzzle with which to work.

Second, individual members' actions that are causing themselves and other members pain are usually based on their faulty perceptions of the actions and motivations of other family members.

The most effective way to change these faulty perceptions is guided contact and discussion with other family members.

> Jim Tarnish is amazed to hear his son tell the therapist that he would like to spend more time with his dad. He even looked forward to the time they had together painting the garage last summer. Jim had been convinced for some time that the kid "hated my guts" and couldn't wait to bolt down his supper and take off somewhere with his friends.

Another reason for seeing the whole family together is so that the therapist cannot be quoted as making fictitious or critical remarks about absent members when the whole family is present. Repeated comments like, "The therapist said your behavior is the cause of our problems," make it unlikely that absent members will become involved in future therapy sessions. Furthermore, no family member can draw the false conclusion that, by being excluded, he is an unimportant member of the family, or that the problem is someone else's fault. Finally, as Laura Dodson (1977) points out in her book *Family Counseling*, problems in a family's interactional patterns, dealt with when the family is together, should help prevent a rerun with another child assuming the "scapegoat" role at a later date.

Many new family therapists find it difficult to get an entire family to meet together about a problem that is discerned as concerning only one member. Or if the whole family does come in, it may be tempting to separate the family for individual therapy because the therapist himself might feel overwhelmed by the destructive process that the family displays in the initial interview. Experiencing ten minutes of a family's unbroken flow of accusations and counteraccusations could make the most seasoned therapist doubt that anything constructive can be accomplished by seeing these people together. But individual therapy, undertaken because a conjoint session might be uncomfortable, generally is doomed to failure. The family's basic problem of how they treat and relate to each other cannot be resolved that way. In addition, families may get the implicit message from such an action that the therapist, too, is frightened of their process and also perceives any possibility of change as being remote.

There may be times as therapy progresses when it is best to meet alone with certain family members to concentrate either on problems in relationships in family subsystems (marital being the most common). When doing therapy with remarried families, separate sessions with one or both of the two original nuclear families that have come together to form the new family may be needed to help this unit deal with unfinished business such as completion of mourning for the breakup of this original family unit. These sessions are best held only after an assessment of the family's interactional patterns and problems has been made with the whole family. Securing the consent of the entire family for these sessions can help ensure every member's continuing emotional involvement in the therapeutic process.

When the involvement of the entire family in therapy is desirable but not immediately attainable, the following approaches may be used.

SEEING VARIOUS FAMILY MEMBERS SEPARATELY

A common procedure is to see parents together and an identified child separately, with siblings possibly included in the latter sessions for limited periods of time. Family members sometimes perceive the therapist as being in coalition with the family member he saw first; therefore, it may be important that the therapist attempt to balance contact with family members by seeing them for approximately the same number of sessions.

If possible, the entire family should meet together before these individual sessions are undertaken in order to secure some agreement on realistic goals the family can work toward in separate sessions. Once these limited goals are reached, an attempt should be made to have the family agree to become involved in conjoint therapy to resolve problems remaining in the total family relationship. This frequently occurs as members become aware that, individually, they cannot solve the family's problems, that therapy is not as threatening as it might have been perceived originally, and that individual actions depend greatly on the actions and interactions of other members of the family.

Occasionally, individual family members may have so much anger and/or emotional blockage toward other members that they cannot tolerate each others' presence in the sessions. Conjoint sessions may only reinforce these negative feelings and family members may choose to leave therapy rather than experience the pain of conjoint therapy.

Courts often order that unacceptable behavior of a given family member be dealt with immediately. If the family is unwilling to be involved in therapy, someone must deal with the juvenile on probation, the child experiencing severe adjustment problems in school, or the institutionalized child. While working in an institution for neglected and predelinquent children, one of the authors noted that following admission, many adolescents refused to see or talk to their families for several weeks. Although many of these youths were experiencing behavioral problems symptomatic of serious family maladjustment, individual therapy was required until the child agreed to participate in family sessions.

INCLUDING ABSENT FAMILY MEMBERS

When, by accident or design, only certain members of a family appear for therapy sessions, a greater sense of the presence of the *entire* family can be created by using empty chairs to represent absent family members in the interview. The therapist then can determine how family members perceive the feelings and attitudes of missing members in certain crucial areas.

Questions such as, "If Dad were here, what do you think he would say about that?" may effectively bring a family member into the session though, in fact, he or she is absent. A member's perception of another member may not be entirely accurate, but the therapist can make a mental note of how an absent member comes across to the rest of the family and the problems this projection may be causing.

Laura Dodson (1977) suggests asking family members who are present to play the role of the missing member, to sit in the empty chair, adopt his or her body postures, gestures, and styles, and respond to comments and questions from the therapist and the rest of the family about the missing person. Dodson believes that the empty chair helps the role-playing member as well as the observers get in touch with feelings the absent member might experience and clarify the attitudes the role-player and the others might harbor toward the absent member.

In the film *Demonstration of a Counseling Session* (see Appendix, p. 166), Alan Leveton suggests bringing absent members into the session by asking each family member to give three words that describe the absent member. Leveton's technique also can be used with all members present. This lets both therapist and family members gain a greater awareness and understanding of how family members perceive one another.

While these approaches are more desirable than delaying needed therapy, it must be emphasized that all family members should be present when therapy begins if possible and that therapy should continue with the whole family until a clear picture of the family's major interactional patterns emerges and some improvement in the total family relationship is accomplished. Dyadal and individual sessions may then be used to work on marital problems, special problems in parent–child or sibling relationships, or individual problems apart from the family relationship.

Where Do You See the Family?

Traditionally, most appointments are scheduled in the therapist's office for reasons such as client expectation or therapist comfort and convenience. A tightly scheduled appointment book rarely provides the luxury of 20 minutes' travel time to and from the clients' home for a session. In family therapy, however, this tradition is unfortunate because it robs the therapist of a rich source of information: seeing where a family lives, how members express themselves through their home and its furnishings, and how they interact in their own setting.

Seeing families at home allows small children to express themselves in more spontaneous and uninhibited ways. They can participate in sessions as they wish. The mother or an older sibling is free from a baby-sitting role and can become more involved in the session. Where traveling distances are relatively short, the therapist often can give clients a choice of home or office sessions. Given a choice, families very often choose their homes for therapy sessions. Arrangements must be made to handle interruptions such as phone calls or unexpected visitors, but once this is done the therapist generally is able to form a better picture of how a family interacts on a day-to-day basis at home.

The preference of beginning family therapists to be in their own familiar office setting, particularly when dealing with several people at one time, is understandable and should not be disregarded. The comfort in the session considerably influences the therapist's effectiveness. It is desirable, however, if geography permits, to make at least one visit to the home to enhance the therapist's understanding of the family and its life-style. Donald Bloch's excellent article, "The Clinical Home Visit" in *Techniques of Family Psychotherapy: A Primer* (1973), provides helpful guidelines for such a visit.

How Often Do You See the Family and How Long?

How often should family therapy sessions be held? There is no set rule. The frequency of sessions depends solely on what best meets the unique needs of the family and the therapist.

Family therapy, by its nature, involves several people, all of whom need to express and share feelings and ideas; therefore, therapy sessions may require more time than individual sessions. Ninety minutes is a good median length for a family session, although some may be longer and some shorter as therapy progresses. Whatever time is invested in a session should be justified by productivity.

Often, when agency therapists are tightly scheduled to 50- or 60-minute appointments because of heavy caseloads, an important issue may have to be postponed until a future session. A family in crisis that might profit most from intensive, closely spaced sessions may, because of limited therapy services, have to accept weekly sessions, relying heavily in the interim on its own strengths or other outside resources to resolve crises.

Good results can be obtained by seeing some families on an intensive, very frequent schedule — perhaps two to four sessions a week over a specified period. Follow-up studies of intensive therapy situations indicate that gains generally hold. High emotional involvement and strong motivation for change have caused these families to work harder than they probably would have if the sessions had extended over several months. Families initially may need longer, more frequent sessions to deal constructively with their concerns, but this need usually tapers off as key issues are resolved and families become more capable of solving their own problems.

The First Interview

Most therapists, no matter how experienced, find it hard initially to sort through a family's divergent perceptions to determine what the group actually is experiencing.

Frank, tense and unhappy, is certain that if Margo would quit threatening and screaming at the kids and carry out her punishments in a more logical and determined manner, the problems with the kids would end. Margo, seething with long-held resentment, sees Frank's hours at work as an escape from the whole miserable situation at home. She is sure the kids act up because they have no guidance and attention from their dad. Hank, tousle-haired and ambitious, feels picked on. He thinks that if his parents gave him more freedom and let him take a job at the truck stop, things would be better. Ann and Tim are fed up with the bickering at home and are sure that if their parents didn't fight so much, they would probably want to stay home more. They even might help out with some of the chores around the house that they now avoid.

The therapist frequently is faced with mass confusion in his first meeting with a family. He faces a bewildering array of people, perceptions, and purposes. The therapist must create structure and suggest a purpose to make sense out of what initially appears to be a nonsensical situation. In the first session the therapist should try to accomplish the following tasks. First, the therapist should learn the family members' perceptions of why they have come to see a therapist. Next, he or she should begin to establish a picture of the family's interactional patterns and the points where family interaction breaks down and becomes destructive to its members. These observations may be shared to a limited degree with the family if it seems that to do so would be productive. Tasks may be assigned to the family during the initial visit to be carried out at home only if the therapist believes he has a good grasp on the family's interactional breakdowns and if family members seem receptive to beginning corrective action. Assignments are designed to modify a family's destructive patterns and will be discussed in greater detail in Chapter 6.

Laura interrupts her husband whenever he makes a comment that she interprets as putting her in a bad light. The therapist empathizes with her discomfort at being portrayed negatively to someone she has just met, but stresses that everyone sees the situation differently, particularly at this early time in therapy. Because of this, the therapist points out that it is important for all members to get a chance to present their views. The therapist indicates that he will be very interested in hearing how Laura sees things as soon as her husband finishes talking. He then deals with the husband's threats to send the daughter, Jane, to a correctional institution if she doesn't shape up by commenting that the father has mentioned this a number of times. The therapist knows how discouraged the father must feel with the many problems in the family, noting that while institutionalization is an alternative open to the family, it should be considered a last resort. Placing Jane in an institution is something nobody really wants if it can be avoided. The therapist tells the family members that they are here to try to find a better way of dealing with their situation. Jane sits quietly, her dark eyes moving anxiously from Mom to Dad and back.

In addition, during the first session the therapist should give the family an opportunity to become acquainted with him or her as well as letting them know what he or she might be able to offer toward helping them make a decision about whether to continue with therapy.

WHO ARE THE FAMILY MEMBERS?

The therapist introduces herself to each family member. She may question each member about his or her age, position in the family, employment, the grade children have attained in school, which school the children attend, and other routine information. This information may be available prior to the session if the therapist's agency or clinic traditionally requires families to complete information forms. Expansion and discussion of this relatively nonthreatening subject matter, however, helps the therapist break the ice with individual family members. Engaging in small talk for a limited time at the beginning of the session gives the family a chance to see the therapist in a less threatening light while providing the therapist with further information about the family by observing what they say and how they say it.

Noting on the application form that Dad was assistant football coach for a local high school that recently won the state championship, the therapist learned that the entire family shared an interest in sports and enjoyed a weekend together earlier that fall when they attended a professional football game in another state. Everyone seemed to react positively to remembering this event.

The therapist will receive additional information about how family members feel about themselves and other members and about being in the therapy session by observing them, noting how they interact with the therapist and each other, where they sit, and the messages they communicate nonverbally through facial expressions, body stance, and movement.

HOW HAS THE FAMILY MADE THE DECISION TO COME TO THERAPY?

Is the family there voluntarily or was the family made to come in by an institution such as the school or the court? If the latter is the case, giving members a few moments to express their feelings about being "made to do this" may be helpful. The therapist can empathize with their feelings that no one enjoys being made to do something under pressure and establish a beginning bond of understanding with the family.

The therapist should tell the family a little about himself at this point and specifically invite any questions that the family might have about his background or training or how he works with families. Such sharing and openness provides positive modeling for the family.

HAS THE FAMILY HAD PAST EXPERIENCES WITH THERAPY? WHAT WAS THE OUTCOME OF THESE EXPERIENCES AND WHAT DOES THE FAMILY EXPECT WILL HAPPEN HERE TODAY?

Every family member enters therapy with some expectation. It is important to help the family identify as many of these expectations as possible in the first session in order to save both therapist and family later frustration and disappointment. Each member should be encouraged to say what he or she thinks therapy will be like and what hopes and fears are held by each one about the experience.

As part of gaining this information from the family, the therapist must attempt to get a clear picture of the family's past experiences with therapy, for the family's perception of these experiences can have a significant effect on the expectations brought to therapy now. If past therapy experiences have been negative, the family may have a hard time believing that this time will be any different.

The therapist can deal effectively with the family's expectations and questions about family therapy through an empathetic and realistic presentation of what will go on in therapy and what both therapist and family will need to contribute to the experience to make a successful outcome more probable. Therapy might be explained to the family as a process where people:

1.   Express and share feelings in order to gain a greater understanding of each other's perceptions.

2.   Mutually discuss problems and ideas as part of a search for workable, satisfying solutions for the problems the family may be experiencing.

3.   Try new ways of dealing with their problems both in the session and outside of the session under the therapist's guidance.

If the therapist senses that the family holds realistic expectations for the therapeutic experience and is demonstrating a beginning motivation to work on their problems at this point, some or all of the following points might be stressed with them now. Doing this preliminary work with the family before members share their perception of the "problem" can provide good groundwork for looking at what is going on in the family from a rational, less emotional perspective. Such a perspective can greatly facilitate the therapeutic process. The therapist must trust his or her judgment as to whether the family would be receptive to hearing the following information at this time, and would be able to make some sense of it, or whether it would better be presented later in the session:

1.   Every member's active participation in therapy is important. (This point frequently needs to be reaffirmed when the fam-

ily presents its perceptions of the problem by labeling one member as being primarily responsible.)

2.   All family members are unique individuals who have had different experiences in their lives and therefore will not be expected to see every situation, issue, or problem in the same way.

3.   In family therapy, the major focus of the sessions will be on improving the family's relationship rather than drastically changing or "fixing" individual members. (This is frequently a new idea for families and may need further emphasis at a later time.)

4.   Mutual efforts to modify or change some of the things that are causing this family pain will not be an easy task. Frequently, disappointments will follow successes and the proverbial "two steps forward and one step back" may initially be the rule rather than the exception.

The following example illustrates a situation in which, in attempting to help a family clarify its expectations for therapy, the therapist also received some important beginning clues as to how family members perceived the problems in their family:

The therapist asked members of the Fitch family what their expectations were for therapy. Dad expressed the hope that the therapist would be able to "talk some sense into Mitch's head," but then said he hoped maybe the two of them could learn to talk without ending up in a fight. Mom echoed her husband's last comment and added that maybe the whole family might learn to understand each other a little better. Todd wondered why he would have to come to future sessions since Mitch had the problem. Mitch said nothing.

The therapist picked up on Mom's hope that everyone might learn to understand one another better and that some special work might be done to help Dad and Mitch learn how to talk and listen to each other. The therapist informed Todd that he was an important member of the family and that the goal of greater family understanding could not be realized unless he participated. Todd was asked whether he would like to have the family relationship improve. Todd said he would and that he would come to the sessions. The therapist turned to Mitch, now more friendly, and asked if things might go better in the family if people were more understanding of each other. Mitch agreed they would. Would Mitch be willing to help work toward this understanding in some future sessions? He would. The therapist then explained what would go on during future sessions and the importance of everyone's involvement and effort if relationships were to improve. Continuing, she stressed that changes often can be an uncomfortable, even frightening experience. Although it would not always be easy, she felt that with everyone's help, the family could learn how to understand and talk with one another in a more satisfying way, since it was obvious that they cared about each other and wanted a happier family relationship.

WHAT DOES THE FAMILY SEE AS THE MAIN PROBLEMS? WHAT DOES EACH MEMBER SEE AS BEING HIS OR HER ROLE IN CONTRIBUTING TO AND SUSTAINING THESE PROBLEMS?

Each family member might be asked what he or she sees as the major problem or problems the family faces. This approach does not always work, however, since the family may state that the problems experienced are primarily the fault of one or two members. A statement commonly heard early in family therapy serves as a clue that such dynamics are operating: "If only Johnnie could get straightened out, things would be fine with this family." If scapegoating one member in this manner is allowed to continue, the probability of meaningful change in destructive family interactional patterns is virtually nil. The therapist can reduce the threat posed by the "family problem" approach by asking family members questions such as: "What is happening in the family that is concerning you right now?" or "What would you like to see different in the family?" Scapegoating one family member may still occur, but employing this approach to problem identification makes it less likely.

Sharp and Lantz (1978), in their article "Relabeling in Conjoint Family Therapy," deal with additional ways of reducing scapegoating in family sessions and ensuring total family involvement. They suggest stressing the fact that most people have a hard time solving a continuing problem without some help from others. After making this point, the therapist should assess each member's willingness to help the scapegoated family member deal with his or her problems. Using this approach, the therapist will find that family members rarely refuse to continue their involvement in therapy.

Jay Haley (1977) suggests that in the initial interview the therapist speak first to family members who appear to be less involved with the problem, saving those most involved and concerned until later. He emphasizes that the therapist must constantly define the problem in terms of involving more than one member, stressing the involvement of other family members in the problem they believe belongs to only one member by emphasizing the upset, worry, and concern that all of this has caused them.

Haley also points out the importance of an "interactional stage" in the initial session in order to gain further understanding of members' perception of the problem as well as observing how they relate to one another. This stage is initiated when the therapist asks family members whether they would spend some time discussing with each other what is concerning them most about the family right now while he sits by and listens. As the therapist observes this discussion, he notes who talks to whom and what members have little interaction with each other. He also notes how members express themselves and whether any coalitions exist in the family. This "interactional stage" gives the therapist some valuable information on family interaction that can be validated as the session progresses. An example of such an "interactional stage" follows.

> When asked to discuss between themselves the matters of most concern to the family, Al and Jean Fitch and their oldest son, Todd, said nothing but turned their gaze toward Mitch, who squirmed uneasily and returned his brother's stare. Al spoke first, mentioning Mitch's failure to attend school and his misbehavior when he did attend. Jean came to Mitch's defense, turning on her husband and accusing him of giving Todd more time and attention than he gave Mitch. Seemingly surprised by his wife's open attack, Al did not respond directly to her but continued berating Mitch because he refused to follow the rules in the family. He predicted many dire consequences for the boy if he did not "straighten up."

As part of this problem-identification segment of the initial session, it is important to assess what each member sees as his or her part in the family's problems. Asking the following question may prove effective: "While family members generally have good intentions and want things to work out well for their family, usually everyone is involved in the problem in some way. Are you aware of anything you might be doing that helps cause the problem or keeps it from being resolved?"

Answers to this question provide an early indicator of the amount of time and effort that may be needed in therapy. A family that is made up of individuals willing to assume responsibility for their involvement in the family's problems is well on its way to resolving them.

Some of the same information may be secured by asking family members how they feel about being at the therapy session. Some discomfort and uncertainty about therapy may be expected, but a family member who resists excessively in effect tells the other members that he finds it too painful to acknowledge his role in the problem. This attitude indicates the need for an extra amount of effort on the part of the therapist to help that family member move to the point where he or she is able to acknowledge involvement.

HOW HAS THE FAMILY ATTEMPTED TO DEAL WITH ITS PROBLEMS IN THE PAST? WHAT HAS BEEN THE OUTCOME OF THOSE EFFORTS?

Therapists from the Mental Research Institute point out that solutions that family members employ to deal with their problems sometimes have the opposite effect of intensifying and perpetuating these problems. Asking family members to describe how they have tried in the past to deal with their problems or improve the family relationship may help pinpoint some of these "well-meaning but doomed-to-failure" attempts. An important outcome of these explorations with a family may be helping members realize that people in the family who had been seen as not caring had tried to improve things, but in a manner that others either did not recognize or labeled as being something other than an attempt to help. The therapist should help the family see that ineffectual prior problem-solving attempts does not mean that people did not care or were not trying to improve things, but rather that a new approach to the situation is needed. Coping patterns from the past that the family recognizes as being unworkable should, by mutual agreement, be discarded in order to ensure that its current problem-solving attempts will be more productive.

> The therapist asked each member of the King family what seemed to stand in the way of getting things worked out at home. She knew the family wasn't investing time and money in therapy to experience a rerun of what went on at home, but she thought that if the family could identify what hadn't worked before, ground rules might be set up for the sessions to avoid such unproductive mechanisms. Mother quietly mentioned people blaming each other when things went wrong rather than taking responsibility for their part in the problem. Seventeen-year-old Jim said people in the family didn't really listen to each other but were constantly interrupting to air their side of the argument. Other family members agreed that both of these things kept happening and caused problems. They agreed that it would be good to have "no blaming" and "no interrupting" rules for the sessions and that family members should make a special effort not to attack each other and to listen more carefully to one another. The therapist asked if any other rules were needed. Harriette, age eleven, suggested that the family agree not to get mad at anyone when they got home for anything said in the session. Dad admitted he had been upset at Dennis, age eight, after last week's session for saying that Dad never did anything with him. Dad did not agree but realized he should have said something about this in the session. Everyone agreed that all members of the family should be free to say what they were feeling in the session without fear of later punishment. They should be free to express disagreement if they did not see something the same way as another member.

This example illustrates "ground rules" that were agreed upon by the family and the therapist for the sessions. Ideally, families can be helped by the therapist to identify, as the King family did, the interactional patterns that get in the way of their constructively resolving problems at home and can agree not to let those things occur in therapy. Sometimes, however, the therapist will have to set some ground rules during the first session with families who insist on blaming each other for problems and take little responsibility for them. If the blaming cannot be dealt with by the therapist empathizing with the pain and frustration the blamer is feeling and redefining the blaming as a well-intentioned attempt on the part of the blamer to improve things or help the blamer refocus on the strengths and positives of the family, some ground rules may be needed. These rules might involve asking family members to agree to focus on what it is possible for *each* of them to do to improve the situation rather than blaming other people. Members may also be asked to agree not to interrupt when other people in the family are talking. The therapist must be careful not to prematurely introduce such rules in a manner that keeps family members from expressing the pain they are feeling because of what is happening in the family, for these feelings must be expressed before they can be dealt with. It may be preferable to wait and set ground rules only when other attempts to stop blaming or interrupting behaviors have proved to be futile.

An effective family therapist will use himself constantly to model and facilitate more constructive interactional behavior within the family. By intervening at the right times, he will project a quality referred to as "sensitive directiveness." This involves staying in charge of the interactions in the family so people don't get hurt or go off on nonproductive tangents, while also remaining open and sensitive to their needs and feelings.

SECURING A COMMITMENT FOR INVOLVEMENT FROM THE FAMILY

As part of this step, the therapist shares with the family what things he or she believes might be accomplished in further therapeutic sessions, how long therapy might be expected to last, and how often and for how long sessions need to be held. It may be difficult to assess how long therapy will be needed at the first session. The authors have found that five sessions will generally give therapist and family adequate time to assess whether or not therapy can be helpful. Therapist and family might agree to evaluate, at the time of the fifth session, what has been accomplished thus far, what might realistically be accomplished in the future, and whether additional sessions might be productive. Once the therapist shares with family members his beginning perceptions of their problems and what therapy might offer them, they must decide whether they wish to proceed with the sessions, back off, or give the matter further thought. Families who are ordered by the court or school to seek help for their problems may have little choice about continuing, although other choices such as time and place of the sessions may be given to them to facilitate some sense of commitment on their part.

When Another Approach Is Needed with a Family

The model just presented will not work for every family, at least not in the neat, step-by-step format offered. A family entering therapy because of what it perceives as outside coercion may be livid with rage or totally beyond the point of listening to one another. The hurt may be so deep that members withdraw and say nothing because they feel it is hopeless to try to get through to other individuals they believe to be callous and uncaring. The therapist may also be looked on as an enemy.

Perhaps therapy is necessary because the family has an abused or neglected child. The social worker comes to the home rather than having the family go to his office. Such families didn't ask him to come to their home. They don't want him there. They believe he has no right to be there. Why should they cooperate?

What can be done to help these families?

The accusing, blaming family calls for a strong measure of sensitive directiveness. The family members probably have an immense amount of pain and strong feelings that need to be expressed, but in other than the destructive manner they have used in the past.

A therapist facing this situation must act immediately to stop the blaming and attacking behavior that leaves every member feeling helpless and hopeless. The family must establish communication on a more productive level in which one person speaks at a time and each member is encouraged to release, in a nonattacking way, the hurt that festers beneath the anger.

Generally, one of two patterns is displayed when family members communicate with one another in a hostile, attacking manner. One pattern is merely to rehash a family's interactions at home. This expression of frustration is virtually always unproductive and should be interrupted by the therapist and replaced with communication patterns that lead to more meaningful expressions and successful resolution of frustrations.

The therapist may, however, occasionally find family members opening up and expressing their frustrations for the first time in the presence of other family members. They may have previously handled their feelings by silence, avoidance, or withdrawal. This type of situation can present a dilemma for the therapist. Shutting off these much-needed expressions of feelings could force a family member to retreat into characteristically nonexpressive patterns if he or she believes it is neither safe nor acceptable to express opinions openly. On the other hand, an open expression of anger and hostility may trigger similar expressions from other family members and the total family may become enmeshed in a shouting and blaming match that accomplishes little.

A frequently successful approach is to ask the member who is sounding off angrily if he might be interrupted for a moment. The therapist then suggests that as much time as necessary during the session be used for each member to talk about the things that upset him most about the family. Family members thus receive a message that it is appropriate to say what they feel, though some messages may be painful for others to hear. Quickly securing everyone's permission to use this approach, the therapist then returns to the family member who was previously talking and encourages him to continue by summarizing what he has said so far.

An exception to using the "wait your turn" approach comes when *one* family member expresses hurt feelings in such an explosive manner that the therapist believes the member probably will not be able to contain himself or listen thoughtfully to what other family members have to say until he experiences some release of those feelings. Provision for release of this type of anger should be made by the therapist as soon as possible, because it is doubtful that the angry member will participate in an ordered problem-solving approach until he has received some assurance that other people in the family are interested in his feelings.

Resistant families must experience some constructive interaction before the initial session ends if they are to have any desire to return. A special effort should be made to guide family members toward constructive communication patterns once everyone has been allowed to air feelings. Parents can be encouraged to model constructively expressive behavior for their children, or the therapist might sense that another family member can handle the task best initially and call upon that person first. The beginning family therapist should find Carmen Lynch's (1975) article on this subject helpful.

Another frustrating situation involves a family or family member who is withdrawn and/or nonexpressive. The silent family member may feel hopeless about expressing feelings because speaking up hasn't helped in the past. Such silence may cover angry or other churning emotions that he or she is trying desperately to keep from overflowing. On the other hand, it may be a manipulative way for one member to elicit concern from others. In these situations the therapist must try to get the silent member to express verbally the feelings being suggested nonverbally.

Sometimes verbal expressions can be encouraged through a technique taken from psychodrama called "doubling" in which the therapist attempts to put herself in the silent member's place and express what she thinks the person may be feeling and experiencing at a particular amount. This technique is described more fully in Chapter 6.

Sometimes other family members may be asked to express, for the silent member, what they think he might be experiencing and share the feelings they believe are communicated through his body language and facial expressions. The family's sensitivity to, and awareness of, the way in which its silent member chooses to express himself can be of invaluable assistance to a therapist.

Sometimes neither approach works in persuading a silent member to open up. The only choice then is to proceed with the rest of the family and wait until the silent member is ready to participate. During this time, the therapist should check with other members to determine what they perceive the silent member's feelings to be on the family issues that arise. Occasionally a family member will break his or her silence to confirm or deny an observation another family member has made.

When the therapist attempted to find out something about Greg and his interests, the boy's answers were terse and monosyllabic. Later, when the therapist asked Greg what changes he would like to see in the family's life-style, he gave no response other than a hard, steady stare. After three unsuccessful attempts to get Greg to express his feelings, the therapist turned to other family members, who were willing to talk about the family's problems. Returning to Greg about ten minutes later with another question and again receiving no response, the therapist began treating the silent boy as she would an empty chair representing an absent family member, asking others what they thought Greg would say about issues on which everyone's opinion was being solicited. Greg remained silent through two rounds of this type of questioning but glared angrily at his sister when, in response to a question, she said Greg would probably say he didn't have any responsibility for any of the family's problems and that they were everyone else's fault. When his sister was questioned about what everyone had tried to do to improve the situation, she said she didn't know how Greg would answer. She said she hadn't noticed him doing anything to help. At this point, Greg exploded with a torrent of words. He cited his enrollment in classes he hated that his father wanted him to take. He told of trying to talk his friends out of the service station break-in. The therapist explored Greg's comments with him, as well as his feeling that his family only seemed to notice the bad things he did and never gave him credit for the good. Greg remained involved verbally through the remainder of the session and reluctantly agreed to return for a second family session the following week.

When a social worker appears as an uninvited guest at a home because of concern about the welfare of a child, he often discovers that the family has previously been in conflict with society over issues concerning the child's management and care. As a representative of society—from a corrections, social service, or education setting—he generally is distrusted and unwelcome. He quickly learns that his initial encounter with such families is likely to be unpleasant and unproductive.

The therapist may not be welcomed immediately by the family but he can move toward gaining its trust by behaving in an honest and concerned manner. This means the family must be told who he is and the reason he is there. It includes sharing with members of the family any information he might have about them.

The family must be informed of probable changes in living patterns that will be necessary if services offered by the therapist and his agency are to succeed. Suggestions for ways to achieve the changes will be offered. The therapist shows empathy for the family's pain and frustration as well as their past difficulties and disappointments, especially when these disappointments have involved other workers in the "helping professions." The therapist must share his understanding that when someone is emotionally drained and despondent, it is not easy to use good judgment in dealing with children. Finally, the therapist must demonstrate that there is hope, that things can change for the better, and that he can help the family achieve desired changes. He then may help the family choose a small, achievable task to work toward together which, in the eyes of the family, will produce a positive change.

Goals must be defined in the family's terms, not in the therapist's, although the end result may be the same. For example, in one case a mother showed little interest in dealing with her son's truancy or misbehavior in school but was interested in "getting the school off my back." That goal was agreed on, and therapy with the family and appropriate liaison work with the school eventually resulted in achieving both the mother's and the school's goals as the boy began behaving better and attending school more regularly.

Here is another example of a social worker moving a family toward meeting society's goals by helping it first deal with its immediate concerns:

Grace Wilson slammed the door in the face of the new social worker. She was angry, and justifiably so, because her six-year-old daughter had been removed from her home two weeks before when the previous social worker had suspected the child was being neglected. The action was taken without any advance warning or attempts to help Mrs. Wilson with her problems. The new social worker persuaded Mrs. Wilson to let her in and explained why she was there. Her agency had received a complaint that Mrs. Wilson's daughter sometimes was left alone until almost midnight. As expected, Mrs. Wilson angrily denied the report. The worker empathized with the frustration of trying to raise a child alone on a limited income. She learned that the mother was working from 11 A.M. to 7 P.M. as a waitress in a restaurant 25 miles from home. With the extremely cold weather, her old car had failed to start several times. At least twice she had not had the money to call a service station and had to wait until a friend got off work at 11 P.M. to start her car with jumper cables. She thought these were two of the occasions her neighbor had noticed. There were still several unexplained late-night absences, but the worker did not push the point. Instead, she talked to Mrs. Wilson about the need to keep seeing her until her problems could be worked out and the little girl was not being left alone in the evening. It sounded as though Mrs. Wilson had many problems with which the worker might help. The problem of the old car was attacked immediately. The social worker knew another woman who commuted from the town in which Mrs. Wilson worked to her home town around 7:30 every night. The mother, though short of funds, said she probably could take a morning bus to work and ride home with the other woman for less money than she was spending on her car. She encouraged the worker to explore this possibility for her. Her hostility had been replaced by apparent relief when she said good-bye to the worker.

The need for immediate and positive bonding among family members is a primary concern when dealing with angry and resistant families. Individuals must be convinced that other family members care about them and the family relationship before they will be willing to invest energy in that relationship. Members of angry families who do not have meaningful contact with each other rarely believe that anyone cares. The therapist must quickly help individuals experience the caring concern of other family members.

Luthman and Kirchenbaum (1974) talk about the "positive double bind," in their book *The Dynamic Family*, as one way this may be achieved. The basic premise of "positive double bind" involves the therapist stressing to the family that:

1. Its members care about each other.
2. Its members have done the best they know how, even though their efforts have not always worked.
3. Everyone in the family wants to solve the problems, to be happy, and to get along better with each other.

Family members generally will not deny having such intentions and may find that a direct expression of these intentions becomes a motivating factor to help them to begin acting in a more caring manner.

Other bonding techniques, which will be covered in more depth in Chapter 6, include therapist emphasis and guided discussion of the family's strengths and things its members have in common. Mutually enjoyed activities that family members have shared in the past and traits that family members admire in one another are among the positive factors that might be discussed. Family sculptures, particularly integrative ones, also can prove to be a powerful bonding technique; sculpting is described in more detail in the next chapter, on interactional assessment techniques.

Goal Setting with Families

Nearly all families that enter therapy, whether voluntarily or involuntarily, hope their lives will change for the better. Even families submerged in pain and surrounded by hopelessness cling to a desire for things to improve.

Frequently, hoped-for changes are seen as being the responsibility of other family members. Initial goals that family members bring to therapy tend to reflect each member's desire for the therapist to be an ally in changing the behavior of others. They may show little awareness of the causative relationship between how everyone in the family interacts and the unhappiness they are all experiencing.

Asked what he would like to see different in the family, Harry said he would like to have his sons do things he asked of them without a lot of back talk. Without the therapist's gentle interruption, turning the question to another family member, he probably would have cited several instances of the boys' misbehavior and disrespect toward him, followed with a comment, "Kids today have no respect for their parents. When I was a boy . . ." His conclusion might be something to the effect that, "If those kids would listen to me half as well as they do to their lousy friends, we wouldn't have any problems."

Early in the therapeutic relationship the family must be helped to establish goals toward which everyone is mutually committed to work. Attainment of these goals requires the effort and involvement in therapy of all family members; a "repair job" on one or two family members isn't enough. Agreeing upon interactional goals—learning to talk and listen to each other more effectively, learning how to avoid violent screaming arguments, and finding time to spend together constructively—virtually assures joint commitment and involvement. The therapist moves families toward these kinds of interactional goals when possible, rather than establishing goals such as "making Sally listen better," or "having Ben spend more time at home." Achieving the more important interactional goals should create a strong probability of attaining the simpler goals of family members.

Mutual goal setting necessarily involves *soliciting* from all family members the things they would like to see different in the family, then combining those wishes into some common goals. Some family therapists work primarily with the complaint a parent brings in and do not take the time needed to set mutual goals. The authors believe that this is a very risky course of action for a *beginning* family therapist. Perhaps a parent's perception of what is wrong or what needs changing is only part of the problem as far as other family members are concerned. Other members must be encouraged to offer their wishes and observations about the family; otherwise, the therapist risks losing their commitment and involvement in future sessions.

An effective way to move toward setting mutual goals, if the family is not in agreement about what needs to be changed, is to ask each member to make a list of several positive interactional conditions he or she would like to see in the family. This list must be as specific as possible, and each person making a list should indicate how he or she believes other members might behave if the desired conditions were present in the family. For example, the specific types of behaviors that constitute family members' getting along better with each other must be clearly spelled out. This gives other members something definite to respond to in deciding whether these goals are possible and helpful. They also are encouraged to think of additional types of behavior that might move the family toward attaining the desired goal.

After everyone has completed a list, each family member is asked to share his or her list with the group. As a member reads each item on his or her list, the therapist should check with other family members to determine:

1. If they, also, see this condition in the family.
2. What obstacles they see preventing this condition from occurring.
3. What would they be willing to do to help this condition to come about.

A further extension of the goal-setting process involves exploring dyadal relationships between family members. One family member might be asked whether something is lacking in his relationship with another member and if he would like to see the situation improve. The other member then is asked to respond. She is asked whether the condition does, in fact, exist, whether this is something she, too, would like to improve, what obstacles she perceives in attaining this goal, and what changes the two might be able to bring about by working together. Obviously, this approach is unnecessary if conflicts and disappointments between all family members are adequately identified during the mutual goal-setting process.

An alternative approach to goal setting is to ask family members at the end of the first session whether they will sit down at home during the week, discuss what they want their family to be like, and bring their conclusions back to the next session. At this point, families may be unable to reach agreement without the assistance of a third party. When this happens, the therapist can spend the second session helping the family set its goals. The manner in which the family deals with the task provides valuable information on how effectively its members communicate with each other and helps identify some of the barriers to productive problem solving.

Goal setting takes time, and if therapeutic contacts are limited, some short-cuts may have to be taken, such as listing only one or two desired interactional conditions by each member.

Throughout this process, the therapist acts as facilitator, coordinator, and recorder, combining similar family wishes and concluding the discussion with a summary of the conditions the members have agreed they want to work toward. Family members then are asked to establish goal priorities and to decide which goal they want to pursue first. Information from family members concerning their perception of barriers to the attainment of family goals, as well as things they see themselves being able to do to help reach these goals, can be filed away for future reference.

> The three lists prepared by members of the Gelke family showed that everyone wanted to spend more time together in recreational activities, to have fewer arguments, and to be able to discuss problems and arrive at solutions with which everyone could live. The family agreed that the last two conditions were closely related and agreed the place to start was to "learn to solve our problems in ways that don't cause family members to feel hurt and angry."

Situations in Which Family Therapy May Not Be Effective

Unfortunately, a family's commitment at the conclusion of the initial family therapy session to participate in additional sessions does not automatically ensure a positive outcome. Some families lack the energy, motivation, and organization to involve themselves in the rigorous and demanding experience of conjoint family therapy. The prognosis for significant, positive change to occur through the conjoint family therapy approach is greatly reduced when certain conditions are present in a family.

For example, if the family cannot commit itself to consistency in attending family sessions and frequently cancels or reschedules appointments, therapy is not being given a chance and cannot work. An inconsistent attendance pattern does not permit issues to be followed through to resolution, and the therapist ends up expending a disproportionate amount of energy wondering whether the family will be available to follow up on vital concerns.

Second, some family members either refuse to participate or are sporadic in their attendance. Total family involvement is especially important in the initial assessment stages of therapy to help the therapist identify family processes and deal with relationship issues. Randy Roberts (1982) presents a number of helpful suggestions in the *Journal of Marital and Family Therapy* for working with parents if the member refusing to be involved in the sessions is a rebellious older child.

Family therapy may not be effective when one or more family members consistently refuse to acknowledge individual responsibility for any part of a family's problems. Members must move beyond blaming others and accept their own involvement in the family's current situation. When one or more family members delegate responsibility for solving the family's problems to the "therapist expert" or demand that another family member change first, refusing to acknowledge that there is anything they can or should do to help the situation, therapy will not be helpful. Problems also arise when one or more family members seem unable to acknowledge *any* caring feelings toward other members or identify anything about the others that they admire.

If the parental subsystem is so weak that it is virtually nonfunctional, family therapy will likely fail. These people may have lost almost all ability to communicate or to function cooperatively and are unable to provide even minimal leadership to their "team." In such families, conjoint marital therapy with the parents (either prior to or simultaneously with family sessions) may be a prerequisite to any possibility of a successful outcome in work with the family.

When severe mental illness is present in one or more members of the family, conjoint family therapy will be fraught with extra problems. Although many highly-skilled family therapists have been successful in treating families with mentally ill members, the beginning family therapist should seek continuing psychiatric consultation when working with such a family.

Finally, if the family demonstrates a continuing pattern of seeking out a variety of "experts" with whom it can share its problems and from whom problem-solving advice may be solicited, family therapy may not be of any use. Frequently, such families consult several helping persons simultaneously. If the therapist finds himself working with such a family, his counsel will be thrown into a pot with all the other experts the family is consulting. In such situations, engaging the family in an orderly plan of change to which all members are committed is virtually impossible.

These conditions need not be viewed as insurmountable if they appear in initial sessions with the family, with the possible exception of the suspected presence of severe mental illness, which requires immediate medical consultation. The beginning family therapist needs to be aware, however, that if these conditions continue to manifest themselves in succeeding interviews, the impediments they create to therapeutic progress must be discussed with the family. Such a discussion will, hopefully, provide a mutual decision as to the wisdom of continuing with family therapy as the treatment of choice for the family's problems.

5
CLARIFYING THE FAMILY'S INTERACTIONAL PATTERNS

Therapists often are frustrated when a family's interactional patterns remain unclear after several sessions. Family members may not respond spontaneously to each other because of the newness of the situation, their discomfort with being in therapy, anger, pain, discouragement, or their mistrust of the therapist. The therapist may wonder whether he sees the full extent of the family's dynamics or if the family has a wider repertoire of actions upon which to draw. The therapist may experience mounting frustration when, despite his or her best efforts, the family continues to blame or make one member a scapegoat rather than examining objectively the group's overall responsibility for its problems, or when the family refuses to connect the scapegoat's behavior and the interplay between that member and the rest of the family. Mutual goal setting may have broken down or may proceed with great difficulty.

The answer to these dilemmas is frequently the same: mutual discussion and/or involvement of the family in experiences designed to help make its interactional patterns more apparent to everyone. Three types of activities that can be used to help a family clarify its interactions will be described in this chapter. Ways in which a family's past can be used productively to help them better understand their present interactions also will be examined.

Activities That Illustrate the Interactional Process

THE FAMILY DRAWING

Equipped with a large box of crayons and large sheets of paper or pasteboard, the family therapist can derive some helpful insights into a family's interactional process with a project that most families find enjoyable. The family's task is simple and requires only a few words of instruction. The therapist asks each member to draw on a single shared sheet of paper, without talking to each other, a picture of anything they wish (see Fig. 11). A more limited "process picture" of important events in a family's life may be attained by asking members to draw a picture of important days or times they have experienced together — perhaps a picture of last Christmas, or Dad's birthday, or a favorite vacation, or a particular time when everyone was upset or angry.

Eva Leveton (1976) states that valuable clues concerning a family's interaction can be gained by observing:

1.   Who started the drawing? How did other members react to that action? Does this member typically "take charge" in the family?

2.   How did family members use and share their space on the paper? Did the family share in achieving certain goals related to how one member was perceived to have intruded on another member's space or perhaps how a member clearly staked out a part of the drawing as being "his territory"? Did any member seem to confine himself to the edges of the drawing or to resist involvement? Were these actions typical of how members fit into and move within the family structure at home?

3.   How did family members communicate in completing the drawing? Were these patterns typical of the family's daily interaction? How did family members communicate good feeling toward one another? How did family members behave when they disagreed or felt angry about something another member did? How did family members behave when they felt imposed or intruded on by a particular family member and wanted him to stop what he was doing? How did the family attempt to get a single member to do something it wanted him to do?

The family drawing generally is completed in a short time. It may be followed by additional drawings if the therapist believes additional information will help to more clearly define the family's interactional process.

The therapist then leads a discussion about the completed family drawing. The discussion can begin with each member being asked to relate how he or she experienced completing the drawing. Each

Figure 11.   The family drawing is an extremely useful tool for observing family process. Its creative capacity allows all members to participate and encourages the family to share in a nonverbal manner.

member's response, coupled with the therapist's observations, should help the family to examine these issues:

1. Who takes responsibility in the family? Who generally is in charge?
2. How does the family deal with differences of opinion?
3. How does the family communicate hurt, anger, joy, and caring?
4. Does any member feel left out? How does he or she feel left out?
5. How close or far apart do family members feel toward one another?
6. To what extent are individuals allowed to express their unique qualities?

Leveton (1976) suggests that the family drawing also can be used to help families work on portions of the interactional process with which they are having problems. The family might be asked to express in the drawing the manner in which it fights and makes up. Or each member might be asked to express through her part of the drawing those things she believes makes her special and unique from other people.

> Gen, 36, and Todd, 35, have been married a year and a half. Ann, 13, and Tim, 5, were born to Gen in her first marriage. The children began the sketch by drawing a house. Gen and Todd stood awkwardly nearby. Gen soon recognized the house as the one she and her former husband occupied with the children. Ann placed a figure behind the house that she later identified as her "real dad." Gen handed Todd a crayon, silently inviting him to participate. Ann began drawing three stick figures in the upper right-hand corner of the drawing. The figures could be identified as two females and a smaller male. Gen drew a picture of two parents and two children in front of the house. Todd added shrubs and a sidewalk. The drawing graphically illustrated problems Todd was experiencing in being accepted into the family by the children and Gen's continuing and frequently frustrated efforts to bring

him and the children closer together. The four people began talking about their individual difficulties in feeling part of the new family. Everyone was able to look at some of the things they had been doing that were driving family members further apart. For the first time, Ann admitted that she could see how her misbehavior had driven a wedge between her mother and stepfather in deciding how to deal with her.

The family drawing can also be used to include disinterested or uninvolved young children in a discussion that primarily involves older members and the therapist. Young children are given paper and crayons and asked to make a drawing of their family on their own or with the other children. The children are asked, when the opportunity presents itself, to share their drawings with other family members and the therapist. This exercise provides a diversion for the children and gives the family and the therapist an opportunity to gain some understanding of the family's interactional patterns from the perspective of its youngest members.

THE FAMILY SCULPTURE

A popular process assessment technique in family therapy is the family sculpture (Fig. 12). Family sculptures represent another example of an action technique through which family members can, without words, demonstrate their interactions. Like the drawing, this technique can be especially productive with children, with families that have limited verbal skills, or with families that hide behind words as a way of masking and denying feelings.

Every family member is asked to allow himself or herself to be used in creating a living sculpture that will help provide a clearer understanding of some of the things that are happening within the family. The therapist then selects a particular family member to do the sculpture. The selected person may be perceived by the therapist as being particularly sensitive to family interaction and probably able to be creative in expressing that sensitivity. On the other hand, the chosen person may be scapegoated or otherwise feel left out of family matters, and need to communicate his or her pain to other family members. Alternatively, the sculptor might be a respected,

Figure 12.   The family sculpture is an excellent way to animate a family's process. Because of its visual power, the family sculpture can quickly reach the emotional core of a family.

well-thought-of member whose interpretations of family dynamics is likely to be noticed and accepted by other family members. Both adults and children are equally suitable to serve as sculptors.

The chosen person is asked to pretend that every family member is made of clay and that he or she is an artist selected to make a sculpture depicting his or her perspective of the family. The rest of the family is asked to participate in the task without conversation, though the sculptor is free to discuss what he or she is doing with the therapist.

The sculptor is asked to do the following:

1. Place family members as close to or as far away from each other as he perceives them to be, bearing in mind that he will be the last figure to be placed in the sculpture.

2. Each member's posture, arm and leg positions, facial position and expression, and other nonverbal manifestions of feelings are shaped in ways the sculptor believes are particularly typical and characteristic.

3. Figures are placed so they touch each other or otherwise express physical closeness or distance in ways that seem particularly appropriate to the sculptor. Sometimes the sculptor does this spontaneously. Specific instructions should not be given unless the sculptor seems hesitant or appears puzzled about how to express "linkages" between certain family members.

The therapist generally carries on a limited discussion with the sculptor while the sculpture is being completed. The sculptor may be asked to clarify the way certain parts of the creation are shaped. If the sculptor hesitates, he may need encouragement to proceed in expressing his perception of the family. The therapist should keep her conversation to a minimum and should not interfere with the sculpture if it seems to be proceeding in a manner that is expressive of the sculptor's perceptions.

The sculptor is asked to place himself as the final figure in his creation, indicating where he believes he fits in the family. He is told to pay attention to his proximity to other members, physical linkages, and his own nonverbal expression of how he feels about being a member of the family. Before placing himself in the completed product, the sculptor may be asked to assign a sentence to each family member that would express what that person might typically say to him, the sculptor.

The sculpture completed, the therapist encourages each family member to share feelings concerning the position in which he or she was sculpted and asks each person to verify or modify the sculptor's perception. Members who have received a sentence from the sculptor are asked whether the words are appropriate. Members who don't believe the words fit are asked for more appropriate descriptions.

Valuable process awareness usually emerges both from this exercise and from subsequent discussion. Family members benefit from the open communication and sharing of feelings that the exercise generally produces. These results also make the family sculpture a valuable therapeutic tool as well as an interactional process assessment technique in situations in which the therapist is attempting to encourage meaningful communication between family members. Family members consistently report a greater awareness of the feelings of other members, in addition to feeling closer to each other, after experiencing this exercise.

Depending on the amount of time available, a family's desire to participate, and the amount of interactional awareness the therapist feels would be beneficial to the family, other family members can be asked to sculpt the family. Sometimes instead of having another family member do an entirely new sculpture, the therapist asks the new sculptor to perform "corrective surgery" on the first sculpture to make it fit his or her perception of the family better.

Many issues within the family, both painful and pleasant, may be brought out through the use of family sculptures. An in-depth exploration of these issues may be neither appropriate nor immediately desirable if the sculpture is used primarily for interactional assessment rather than as a treatment technique. The therapist must be particularly careful not to allow family members to express more feelings of hurt and pain than can be dealt with effectively in a given session. Everyone's awareness that these feelings exist may be enough. The therapist's ability to constructively facilitate and direct the family's discussion about its experience with the sculpture is crucial. The therapist can prevent too many feelings from coming out too soon by recognizing and briefly summarizing each member's statements and feelings, with a promise that they will receive more attention later.

A family member often is asked, at the completion of a family sculpture session, to make an integrative sculpture of "what he would like the family to be like." Families whose members have indicated an ability to express some positive feeling toward each other often can end the session with this kind of sculpture, promoting a feeling of closeness, understanding, and hope. *

---

* There are a myriad of possibilities for utilizing family sculptures. For further information on this topic, the reader is referred to *Family Counseling* by Laura Sue Dodson (1977), *Children in Trouble* by Eva Leventon (1976), *Primer of Family Therapy* edited by Donald Bloch (1973), *The Marriage Savers* by Joanne and Lew Koch (1976), *Family Therapy* by Philip Guerin (1976), and numerous journal articles (especially those by Peggy Papp and Ellen Wachtel's article in the July 1982 issue of the *Journal of Marital and Family Therapy*).

The Norris family consisted of Carl, 43, Marie, 38, Jim, 17, Pete, 12, and Linda, 11. The family had been referred for family therapy after Pete's serious and repeated misbehavior in the classroom. The family also was concerned about Jim, who had been picked up twice for marijuana possession, had dropped out of school about four months previously, and had not been able to find a job. The family was extremely angry with Pete for "causing them to be in therapy" and seemed unable to empathize with his pain and frustration over poor school achievement, rejection by his peers, and continuing criticism by all family members. Carl and Marie thought his behavior was "deliberately done to humiliate and antagonize them." They agreed to allow Pete to do a sculpture after the therapist briefly explained the purpose of the exercise. Pete was reluctant and needed considerable encouragement from the therapist to proceed. He finally created a sculpture that placed his mother and Linda side by side, holding hands, and his father slightly behind them with one hand on Linda's shoulder. Dad was rarely home because of work commitments and community involvement, and the parents were experiencing some marital strain. Jim was placed slightly behind and to the left of his mother, who tended to come to his rescue in arguments with his father concerning his behavior. Jim did not have physical contact with any other family member. When asked to place himself in the sculpture, Pete stood uncomfortably for a moment and finally went to a chair on the other side of the room and sat down. The sculpture vividly pointed out the separation people were feeling from each other in the family, which they later affirmed verbally. Everyone expressed surprise that Pete felt so totally alone. When Dad later was asked to do a sculpture of how he would like things to be in the family, he placed Pete next to him with his hand on Pete's shoulder. Pete's role as a scapegoat diminished significantly after this session.

THE STRUCTURED FAMILY INTERVIEW

The structured interview was introduced by Paul Watzlawick in the September 1966 issue of *Family Process* and is considered a vintage family process assessment technique. Laura Dodson (1977) also presents the technique, with some variations, in her book *Family Counseling*.

The interview consists of a series of structured family tasks assigned by the therapist, followed by a discussion of how members experienced the tasks and what they learned about themselves and their family by participating. Therapists from the Mental Research Institute in Palo Alto, California, estimate that this technique could give an interviewer diagnostic material on a family's interactional patterns that would take from five to ten hours to obtain through conventional interviewing. The interview frequently follows this format:

1.   Family members are seen separately by the therapist, who asks them to identify what they perceive as the family's main problem. One approach that may be less threatening is to ask, "If there was one thing you could have different in this family, what would it be?" This avoids the "we have no problems" response. Other family members wait outside, and after each family member is assured that his or her response will be confidential, the family spends five to ten minutes discussing the question together. The therapist sometimes can begin the discussion with a personal observation that each family member seems to have a somewhat different perception of what should be changed to improve family relationships. This exercise can demonstrate how open a family is in discussing painful issues and the patterns they use in dealing with differences. It sometimes discourages scapegoating when individual problems are redefined as family problems.

2.   Family members are given a few minutes to plan an activity they might enjoy doing together. The therapist either sits in a corner of the room or goes outside and observes the family through a one-way mirror. Families also can be broken into smaller groups, such as parents, and child or children, and the exercise is repeated. Observed family interaction can offer clues to the degree experiences are shared, the potential for future shared experiences, and strengths on which to build family relationships. The manner in which the family deals with differing wishes and preferences also can be assessed.

3.   The children are asked to leave the room and the parents are asked, "How did you, of all the people in the world, get together?" This exercise can demonstrate hopes and expectations each

partner brought to the marriage, how they perceive their relationship, and some of the patterns they follow in interacting as husband and wife.

4. The parents are asked to teach their children something. The therapist gives each parent a card on which is written, "A rolling stone gathers no moss." The couple is asked to discuss the proverb for five minutes, reach some agreement on its meaning, and then call in the children and teach them its meaning. The therapist observes but does not participate in this exercise. The exercise reveals the manner in which the parents handle their differences and how they convey information to their children, particularly if the parents are in disagreement. Family coalitions also may be highlighted. For example, a child may be asked to give his interpretation of the proverb; one or both of the parents may automatically agree, or if the idea is advanced by a scapegoated child, one or both parents may instantly disagree. Generational conflicts also may emerge around the desirability of "moss gathering."

5. How do people in the family perceive each other? The family remains together and each member is given two cards. On the first card each is asked to write what she thinks is the main fault of the person sitting to her left, without identifying either herself or the person about whom she is writing. Each member is asked to repeat the procedure on a second card, this time indicating what each likes most about the same person. The therapist may add one or two cards he has written that may seem especially appropriate for the family. The therapist collects all of the "Fault" cards, mixes them together, adds his own cards and reads them aloud. The therapist may reword the cards to disguise identifying factors while maintaining the original meanings. For example, "She nags too much" may be changed to read, "This person tries too hard to get other people to do what she wants them to do." "He's mad all the time" might be read as, "This person is upset much of the time." Each family member is asked to identify whom he thinks each card best describes. The same family member should not be the first to be asked, "Who was this card written about?" each time. Rather, the task should be rotated with each card in order to identify potential leaders and followers or to detect any family alliance patterns. The therapist should insist that family members narrow their guesses down to one individual if they say they don't know or can't decide which member a card describes. Through this exercise, scapegoating

patterns can be detected, problems brought into the open, and family members' perceptions of one another laid open to scrutiny. The openness of family communication also can be assessed. Frequently, a family member denies having written a critical card about another member by stating that he thought the card he wrote was about someone other than the person on his left. This obviously implies that another member wrote the card. Repeating the exercise with the positive cards brings out strengths on which to build as well as constructing a picture of how members reinforce one another's self-concept. Individual family members also can gain some positive reinforcement and hopefully will complete the exercise on a positive note.

The structured interview can be concluded at this point. The therapist can then initiate a discussion concerning how individual members experienced the exercise. Additional tasks can also be added to other tasks substituted for those described that might, in similar or better ways, pinpoint family interactional patterns. Virginia Satir assigns an additional task during the process that offers valuable information on how people perceive themselves and the reality of their perceptions. She asks each family member to state:

1. What would you say is your main fault?
2. What do you admire most about yourself?

Using Family History to Understand Family Interactions

Learning how two people came together to begin a family, what kind of preparation they had for assuming the roles of spouse and parent from their families of origin, and the kinds of experiences they have had in trying to create and sustain their family unit can provide the therapist with additional insight into a family's process. She may learn about the patterns of coping and interacting with one another and the world at large that the family appears to be utilizing, the manner in which these interactional patterns got started, and what sustains them.

Generally the authors question the value of devoting several therapy sessions to discussing family history in detail, unless past experiences seem unresolved and are seriously interfering with the family's present functioning. Following is an example of how the dynamics of a family origin were interfering with the present family's functioning.

> During the second session, Lorraine expressed anger toward what she perceived as her husband "putting his own family ahead of us." She complained about his immediate responses to frantic phone calls from his mother, who demanded that he come over several times a month to settle fights between his brother and father. Sensing his wife's displeasure, he began lying about where he was going, only to find his wife further infuriated when she discovered where he had been.

The family therapist's first clue about problems from the past that are interfering with a family's present functioning and future growth often comes from taking a limited family history near the beginning of the therapeutic process, including the following.

Characteristics of the Parents' Families of Origin / These characteristics might include information on their parents' marital relationship, parent–child relationships, sibling relationships, the present role of the parent in his or her family of origin, how feelings and emotions were expressed in the family, how differences were handled, the emotional climate of the family, and the nature of the present relationship that the client or family has with both of the spouses' original families. The family of origin is crucial in teaching its children what options are open to them in relating to a spouse in a marital relationship and to a child in a parental relationship.

The Marital Relationship of the Parents in the Family / Try to ascertain how the husband and wife got together, their hopes and expectations for their relationship, their disappointments and adjustments, and the nature of their current relationship, including quality and quantity of marital time shared. The therapist also may want to identify prior marital and/or "love" relationships on the part of either spouse and the way these relationships may have influenced the present marital relationship. The reinforcements and satisfactions that parents derive from the marital relationship will critically affect their parenting abilities and the learning model they present their children as they grow toward becoming spouses and parents.

Prior Experiences of the Family at Times of Crisis / Times of typical crises include the conception and birth of children, children entering school, and adolescence. Times of nontypical crises include serious illness, disease, death, addition or loss of family members, separation, and excessive changes in jobs or residences. The therapist must note how the family handled these kinds of experiences. Faulty interaction processes frequently have their origin in such experiences.

Some history-taking is essential in dealing with single-parent families and remarried families. Family members often can share, for the first time, the pain that they experienced when the original family broke up and that they may have never discussed before with each other. Each member has an opportunity to discuss the difficulties experienced in trying to fit into a new family. Some attention should be given to the things members like about the new family and the potential for positive sharing between family members.

FAMILY OF ORIGIN SESSIONS

Exploration of family history may indicate that parents still have "unfinished business" with their families of origin that is interfering with their present functioning both as individuals and as family members. Old hurts may need to be discussed and resolved or relationships with their families of origin may need to be redefined in a more mutually satisfying manner. Sometimes these matters can be dealt with only by bringing in selected members of the parent's family of origin for a few sessions with their child. These sessions are generally conducted in one of two ways.

Some therapists choose not to meet with the parent and members of the family of origin but will rather provide the family member with special training and rehearsal experiences so that he (or she) will be able to go back to his family of origin and deal with painful issues with them on his own. Murray Bowen's work (1978) is especially helpful when using this approach.

Another approach involves the family member and appropriate members of his or her family of origin meeting with the therapist to discuss the necessary issues and do the necessary preliminary work in restructuring the nature of the member's involvement with his or her present family. The adult child may initially show strong resistance to participating in such a meeting with parents. This resistance is generally borne out of earlier, distorted perceptions the child held of the parents and may be expressed by statements such as "They'd never agree to come to something like that" or "I couldn't talk to them like that. It would hurt them too much." James Framo (1976) suggests that this resistance may be overcome by continuing encouragement from the therapist, which may include confronting the adult child with the fact of the parents' inevitable death and the need to get these matters resolved before this happens. Once the child agrees to a session with members of his or her family of origin, preparatory sessions will be held with the therapist that may include identifying issues to be brought up in the family of origin sessions as well as rehearsing ways of presenting and dealing with these issues.

Although the family member will probably be asked to introduce and direct the discussion of these issues with his or her family of origin, the therapist can provide crucial support, security, and direction in the session to everyone present. Sessions involving a member's family of origin are frequently characterized by intense emotional involvement on the part of everyone present. Misconceptions from the past are brought out, discussed, and often resolved. The sessions can provide the impetus for new understanding, appreciation, and closeness between all family members.

Before the therapist attempts to conduct sessions with families of origin, he should become familiar with the works of Murray Bowen (1978), James Framo (1976), Norman Paul (1967, 1975), Al Napier and Carl Whitaker (1978), and Don Williamson (1982), as well as Lee Headley's book, *Adults and Their Parents in Family Therapy* (1977).

THE FAMILY PHOTO ALBUM

A relatively simple and effective way to get some family history in a single interview is the family photo album. Asking the family to share one or more of its albums usually elicits enthusiastic cooperation and gives the therapist an opportunity to observe what events and activities were recorded and which family members were involved.

The therapist should note whether certain members are consistently absent from the photographs. He should be conscious of markedly different physical appearances of certain members, excluding changes attributable to growth, age, and style changes. He must consider whether physical changes may have emotional antecedents. Family members may be asked to describe past events and interactions represented by the pictures. Were these difficult times or were they times more satisfying than the present? Do members of the family have differing perceptions about past happenings that haven't been shared previously?

> The therapist asked the Norris family to share its family photo album during the third session. The album was placed on the coffee table in front of the sofa. Family members gathered around the table and showed considerable interest in viewing the pictures and answering the therapist's questions. The pictures portrayed a number of family outings and vacations that everyone obviously had enjoyed. Mr. Norris said the family hadn't enjoyed a good time together for more than a year. Everyone wished they might again share some good times like those pictured in the album, but the mother's second job and a general tendency for everyone to go off on his or her own had made this all but impossible. Mr. and Mrs. Norris recognized the fact that Mom's second job was not crucial to the family's financial well-being when their son pointed out that the things they used to do together, such as camping and fishing, didn't cost that much money. Mrs. Norris agreed that she probably would be less tired and irritable without the second job and conceded that it would probably be a good idea for her to quit the job. The family planned an outing for the upcoming Memorial Day weekend.

Though sharing a family photo album is most easily accomplished in a family's home, the group can bring the books to the therapist's office when a home visit is not possible.

THE GENOGRAM

The genogram, a simple sketch by a family member or the therapist that can be completed in a single interview with a family, allows the therapist to learn more about both spouses and their families of origin, as well as the functioning and interactional patterns in the present family. Figure 13 is an example of a typical genogram.

This genogram shows that Barbara and Jim Carter were married in 1975. Each had children from previous marriages. Barbara was formerly married to Len; they had two sons, Frank, 16, and Alex, 14. Barbara and Len were divorced in 1971. Len has remarried and has a two-year-old daughter by the new marriage. Jim was formerly married to Kate; they had two daughters, one of whom is now married, and a son. They were divorced in 1974.

Barbara's sons live with her and Jim. Jim's two youngest children live with their mother, who recently remarried.

Barbara was one of four children. One brother and one sister are married, have children, and live on the West Coast. Another brother is divorced and lives in Idaho. Barbara's parents are divorced. Her mother lives in Seattle. Her father lives in the same community as Barbara; he has a drinking problem. Both of Barbara's paternal grandparents are dead. Her maternal grandfather is dead but her maternal grandmother lives in a Seattle nursing home. One of her grandfathers was an alcoholic. Her mother has five siblings, all of whom are living. Her father had four siblings.

Jim was one of four children. An older brother was killed at Normandy. An older brother and a younger sister are divorced. His mother died of a stroke in 1968. His father lives in Denver with his younger sister and her two children from a former marriage. Information on Jim's grandparents is not included.

The therapist was able to ask the family several questions while preparing the genogram. Some of the areas that were found to have direct bearing on the family's present functioning and to need further exploration included:

1.   The boys' feelings about their mother's marriage to Jim.
2.   How the boys and Barbara experienced the first family and its later breakup.
3.   The boys' present relationship with their natural father and their resentment and disappointment because of his limited contacts with them.
4.   The boys' relationship with their stepmother and married half-sister.
5.   The boys' relationship with Jim's children.
6.   Jim's relationship with his stepsons.

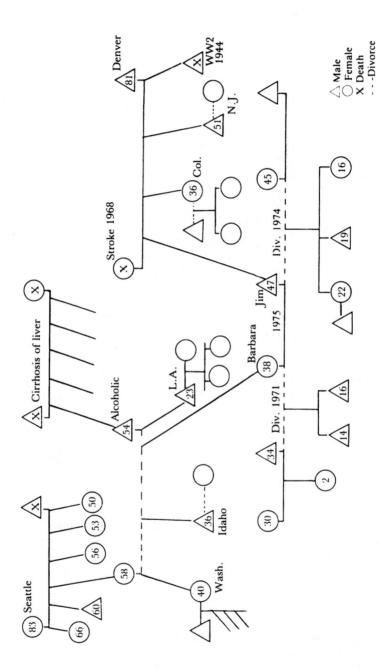

Figure 13. A genogram of the Carter family.

7. How Jim felt about his first family and its breakup; he had little opportunity to work through his feelings about this because he married Barbara shortly after his divorce.

8. Jim's present relationship with his children and his satisfactions and disappointments with the relationship.

9. The present relationship Jim and Barbara have with their former spouses and how those relationships influence their marriage.

10. Jim and Barbara's present relationship with their families of origin and how those relationships influence their ability to function well in their present family. These include Barbara's continuing concern and involvement with her alcoholic father, about whom Jim is becoming increasingly resentful; and Barbara's concern about Jim's social drinking because two of the males in her family of origin were alcoholics. Jim's drinking has caused several quarrels.

11. The absence of role models from the past for stable, satisfying marriages in both families. Jim's parents remained married, though unhappy. Barbara's parents were divorced. Siblings in both families have been divorced.

Wachtel finds that the use of the genograms may produce greater empathy between children and their parents. It often gives children information about their parents and their origins that they never had before. It may help parents who are having difficulty dealing with some age-appropriate behavior in their children remember what they were like when they were their children's age. She also suggests that if parents have little recollection of older relatives they have placed on the genogram, they should be asked what they heard about these relatives from other family members. Their answers may provide an excellent clue to what the family of origin considered appropriate and acceptable behavior. They may also be asked to guess what these relatives might have been like, since these guesses probably constitute what they treat as reality about these relatives anyway.

As part of the discussion of the genogram with the family, the therapist may ask individual members to express their hurts, joys, and future expectations with other family members as well as things they share with the family and ways in which they believe they are unique. The therapist then asks members to share their perceptions of how this member is unique and different from the rest of the family, stressing areas such as interests, beliefs, and values. Finally, to emphasize *bonding* and *linkages* between family members, the therapist asks other members to share their perceptions of the ways this particular member is like others in the group. After the member has had an opportunity to respond to the family's perceptions of him or her, this process should be repeated with every member.

The key to a successful genogram is flexibility. Symbols can be changed or added and additional abbreviated information placed as needed on the drawing. Sometimes genograms are more appropriately drawn by designated family members with the therapist retaining the right to inquire about information included on the drawing.

The genogram takes up less space in a file and provides a more ready reference than an extensive case history. Philip Guerin (1976), in *Family Therapy*, offers helpful information on the use of genograms.

Appropriate Use of
Interactional Assessment Techniques

Interactional assessment techniques need not be used with every family, although some basic family history information is usually helpful. The decision to use interactional assessment techniques with a family depends on whether the therapist is seriously impeded in his work with the family, particularly when setting meaningful goals, because its primary interactional patterns remain unclear. If so, assessment techniques may highlight some obscure interactional patterns. These techniques are also useful when the family's lack of awareness of its interactional patterns, especially the destructive aspects of these patterns, keep it from setting meaningful goals to work toward to improve relationships. In such situations, the use of assessment techniques can provide therapeutic awareness for a family and move it toward making constructive changes in its interactions.

All family interactional assessment techniques cannot be used with equal effectiveness by everyone. Therapists and families have certain ways of expressing themselves comfortably. These may primarily involve dialogue between family members or experiences or action. Therapists on occasion have valid reasons for wanting members to experience their families in different ways, such as directing a highly verbal family toward communicating nonverbally through touching. Unless a therapist believes a family will benefit from such an exercise, however, members should initially be allowed to express themselves in familiar ways. New interactional experiences can be introduced later.

EXERCISES FOR PRACTICING INTERACTIONAL ASSESSMENT TECHNIQUES

The following techniques can be used in training therapists to work with families.

The Family Drawing / Several family therapy trainees who previously have talked together can do a drawing on a large sheet of paper. Do not assign particular roles, and ask participants not to talk while the drawing is being completed. A picture of the participants' relationship should emerge. As with a family drawing, leadership issues will emerge, as indicated by the person who started the drawing and how other people reacted, along with issues of how people shared space and made linkages. In addition, this exercise demonstrates how differences and expressions of individuality are handled, if any member is isolated, and how the group deals with the isolated member. Once these issues are identified and discussed, each participant should be asked to pretend that the group is a family and he is a member. Each member is asked to identify what he believes his role would be in the family and to relate how he feels about being a member of the family. Feelings and awareness expressed by the participants are similar to those real family members might experience in doing this exercise.

The Family Sculpture / Following the identification of family roles and climate in a simulated family drawing exercise, "family" members are asked to create a family sculpture. When the sculpture is done, members are asked to share how they felt about the exercise. Additional sculptures may be made by other "family" members if desired. Participants playing roles in simulated family interviews also may be asked to make a sculpture of their simulated "family," indicating how they feel about the experience. This exercise may have considerable emotional impact on its participants, even when stimulated. Participants gain an opportunity to practice the technique and, at the same time, receive some idea of how a family might experience the exercise.

The Structured Family Interview / Movies and audiotapes of Virginia Satir conducting and discussing an interview are available. Group viewing and listening as well as discussion of interactional patterns can be helpful in learning to use the exercise.

The Genogram / Two participants pair off and take turns drawing genograms of their families with the nondrawing observer asking questions she might typically ask of a family. Used as a group exercise, all of the participants might draw their own genograms. One participant might volunteer his genogram to be used by another volunteer interviewer, who will demonstrate exploration and discussion of a genogram in front of the entire group.

6

DEALING WITH FAMILY PROBLEMS: VERBAL TECHNIQUES, EXPERIENTIAL TECHNIQUES, AND ASSIGNMENTS

Therapist and family have agreed upon the goals they would like to work toward in their sessions together. The therapist has enough understanding of the family's interactional patterns to identify which of these interactions need to be modified or changed as part of the process of meeting these goals. Together, therapist and family are approaching the core of the therapeutic process where, under the therapist's guidance, positive steps will be taken toward making the interactions of the family more productive and satisfying for its members.

As part of this process, the therapist will utilize a variety of techniques such as those described in the following pages, and family members will gain new understanding and perceptions of both their own and other family members' feelings and behavior. Just how much "awareness" on the part of the family as to why they are doing what they are doing is necessary for change remains a controversial subject in the field of family therapy. The authors believe that in participating in the therapeutic experience, certain perceptual changes in how a family views itself and its problems almost always occur, whether or not these changes are ever discussed.

Change is uncomfortable for both families and individuals. Despite a family's expressed desire to feel better, the period in therapy when significant family changes begin to occur may be fraught with setbacks and frustrations for both family and therapist.

The techniques of intervention used during this stage of family

101

therapy are verbal techniques, experiential techniques, and assignments.

Emphasis has been placed on the use of verbal techniques in the section on the beginning interview. Experiential techniques were introduced in the section on understanding family process. The three types of interventions are dealt with in more detail in the following material.

VERBAL TECHNIQUES

At this stage of therapy, family members should be talking to one another, although largely under the therapist's direction. Some of this discussion may involve family members exploring painful interactions from the past that remain unresolved and continue to produce strong feelings as well as barriers to closeness between family members. Some of the discussion will center on what is happening between family members in the here and now and involve sharing feelings and differing perceptions about these processes. Some of the discussion will focus on the search for better ways of dealing with problems than the family has utilized in the past and the family's hopes and dreams for the future. The therapist can facilitate discussion between family members by offering encouragement to members to express their opinions and feelings as well as to listen to similar expressions from others. He offers clarification of feelings and ideas that seem unclear to other family members and guides the discussion between members into productive channels. He may also share his own feelings and observations about what is happening or has happened in the family. This is the technique that therapists rely on most heavily and that they must ultimately utilize in helping families make sense of and learn from experiential techniques and assignments that they will participate in.

EXPERIENTIAL TECHNIQUES

Sculptures and family drawings are examples of experiential techniques. These techniques may sometimes be more successful than talking in helping a family understand its processes and/or feelings. The family's resulting awareness may serve as a lever to move the family toward change. Experiential tools are especially valuable with families that have trouble talking about their feelings. Experiential techniques can provide a release valve for families whose feelings are running high and who face an explosive situation because of pent-up emotions. Family members who are able to discharge their feelings first through controlled physical activities generally find that they can then talk about these feelings much more easily. Verbal techniques limit participation, but experiential techniques involve the entire family, including young, less verbal children. Experiential techniques may provide an element of fun or play that bonds family members in a positive way. Some families may not be comfortable with experiential activities, though the therapist's discomfort with these activities rather than the family's frequently is the reason the techniques are not used or are used unsuccessfully.

ASSIGNMENTS

Assignments with both verbal and experiential components help families try new behaviors during the week. Assignments, discussed later in detail, generally involve: (1) reversing present behavior; (2) making small changes in the way family members interact; or (3) continuing to perform a designated "problem behavior," but under altered circumstances. A 60–90 minute conversation with a therapist once a week seldom provides a family with sufficient impetus to change a situation. Therapy must be a continuing process in which a family is involved between sessions. Assignments increase a family's confidence in its ability to function well independently of the therapist, a belief that is essential to the family's future growth.

Read this example and think of ways the therapist might help the Drew family bring about the changes necessary to reach its goals. Repeat the exercise after completing the chapter.

Members of the Drew family include Harry, 44, Beth, 40, Angie, 18, and Tom, 13. The parents initially were very concerned about Tom's two minor skirmishes with the law. They were worried about Angie's overactive social life, her grades in college, which were rapidly deteriorating, and her increasing estrangement from her mother. A goal they agreed to work on in therapy was to seek more enjoyable time together. The therapist observed the following barriers that kept the family from achieving its goal:

1. Angie's "too-busy" schedule was because of her college class schedule, her busy social life, and a part-time job, which required her to work 30 hours a week.
2. Family members found it hard to acknowledge and listen to ideas different from their own. This inevitably produced arguments that caused the members to avoid one another.
3. Previously shared interests such as camping and rock hunting were no longer enjoyed; each member was now involved in his or her own activities, with other members excluded.
4. The children and their father had little to do with each other. Most messages between father and children were delivered by the mother.
5. Father's "too-busy" schedule involved a considerable amount of overtime at work and heavy involvement in volunteer work at his church.
6. Family members, particularly the children, felt themselves to be disappointments to the others. These feelings were intensified by a minimal amount of involvement with each other and interactions that were typically characterized by criticism and blaming.

Chapter 3 described four common process breakdowns that occur in families — communication, self-concept reinforcement, member expectations, and handling of differences. The chapter highlighted some of the unique dysfunctional interactional patterns that can occur and the family climate that is the result of the interplay of these areas. The following ideas can help the therapist deal with these problems. The techniques represent only a sampling of methods that might be tried in family therapy and may be adapted to fit a therapist's individual style and philosophy.

Communication Breakdowns

Problem / People in the family don't say what they're really feeling.

Interventions /

1. Point out the nonverbal contradictions of what someone is saying:

"What is your body saying right now?"

"What do you read from the facial expression of other family members?"

For the most part, people have better control of their verbal behavior than they do of their nonverbal behavior. A person's body mirrors inner feelings. Pointing out contradictions in spoken and unspoken messages of family members aids in self-awareness.

2. Doubling for family members in a session is a psychodramatic technique through which the therapist or a family member attempts to express feelings for a member who may have difficulty expressing feelings (see Fig. 14). The entire family must be made aware of those feelings if a positive change is to occur. Doubling may take the form of the therapist making a simple, empathetic statement for a member such as, "I really think I've disappointed everyone." The therapist continues speaking for the member until the person begins expressing his feelings himself. Doubling may involve the therapist changing her physical position in order to be next to or behind the person for whom she is speaking. The therapist may place her hands on the person's shoulders to convey her support. The therapist should ask permission of the family member in advance to double for him by saying something like this: "I have a feeling you're having a hard time saying some of the things you're thinking. Would it be okay if I sit by you and try to express some of those feelings for you?" The person for whom the therapist is doubling must be assured it is all right, in fact even necessary, to speak out if something the therapist says doesn't describe how the person feels. Doubling sometimes can become a dialogue between the therapist and family member as the member attempts to sort out his feelings and decide the type of action he wants to take.

The technique can be used constructively with an entire family when the therapist senses that feelings are being blocked, thereby inhibiting progress in therapy. Every member of the family is asked to close his eyes; the therapist then attempts to double for each member in terms of how she perceives their feelings. Family members are then asked to open their eyes and talk about how they experienced the exercise. This experience frequently gives people a nudge toward getting back in touch with their feelings. The success-

Figure 14. "Doubling" is an effective method of getting a family member to share feelings that he may be having difficulty expressing. It's a psychodramatic technique in which the therapist or a family member expresses feelings for another member.

ful use of doubling requires a considerable amount of sensitivity on the part of the therapist toward the feelings of the family members involved. Eva Leveton's book, *Psychodrama for the Timid Clinician* (1977), is helpful in understanding and learning to use doubling.

3. Any member's failure to tell other family members what is needed from them or to express his needs and feelings makes it impossible for other members to know what they must do to solve a problem. One exercise that helps bring out feelings and needs involves each person in the family telling every other member directly what he or she needs from them. Then, to facilitate further feeling expression, bonding, and self-concept reinforcement, they are asked to share what they appreciate about the member. A "telling" member may stand directly in front of a "receiving" member to ensure that person is giving his undivided attention to what is being said. This exercise should be continued until everyone has had an opportunity to express needs and appreciation to everyone else. Family members may then be asked to talk about how they experienced the various dialogues and what new information emerged from the dialogue for them.

Problem / People in families lack the skills to express feelings appropriately and openly.

Interventions /

1. The therapist models, through appropriate self-revelation, how feelings such as disagreement, support, uncertainty, and anger are expressed. Helping people get in touch with and appropriately express their feelings remains the cornerstone of any therapeutic process. Increased feeling awareness and expression inevitably lead to more meaningful interpersonal relationships. The therapist's inclusion of himself in the process is extremely valuable in these situations. His modeling sets an example for family members and establishes an atmosphere conducive to feeling expression.

2. The therapist consistently relabels anger as hurt and/or concern and deals with this underlying feeling and its roots. The angry, attacking family member will push other family members further away from him and make sharing and closeness with these members virtually impossible. Relabeling of anger as hurt or concern by the therapist may help the angry member get more in touch with what he or she is really feeling as well as cause other members

to behave less defensively as they understand where the outward expression of anger is coming from. When statements such as "You're a rotten kid" can be relabeled instead to express a parent's concern and worry about a child, mutual understanding and meaningful communication are far more likely to occur.

Problem / Sometimes people in families hesitate to express certain feelings because they fear attack and/or rejection by other members.

Interventions /

The therapist attempts to create a safe and receptive climate in the sessions that promotes open expression of feelings. This might include stopping destructive interactions by establishing ground rules for each session. Such rules generally deal with how family members will express themselves in the sessions and how they will handle outbursts of destructive communication that may occur when they leave. This topic was touched on in Chapter 4.

Problem / Family members do not listen to each other or utilize "mind reading" in their interactions with each other.

Interventions /

1. The therapist models by listening with interest to what each family member has to say and not allowing interruption.
2. The process of using effective feedback techniques that require family members to listen to each other, then repeat what they heard, is continued until both the content and the emotional meaning of a message are reported correctly.
3. "Let's check this assumption out" is useful when a family member attempts to "read minds." The therapist stops him and tells him to describe, in detail, how he reached his conclusion about what another person is thinking and/or feeling. The therapist then has the "mind reader" check with the family member about whom assumptions are made, the correctness of those perceptions and the correctness of the conclusions that came about as the result of the perceptions. Patterns of consistent misinterpretations concerning the behavior of one family member by another member frequently emerge. Teaching a person to ask before assuming is the primary lesson that members should learn from this type of intervention. For further information on dealing with mind reading, the reader is re-

ferred to Bandler, Grinder, and Satir's book, *Changing with Families* (1976).

Problem / Family members fail to communicate directly with other members or utilize "middleman" communication, such as Dad disciplining the children through Mom.

Interventions /

1. The therapist asks participants in the session to talk directly to each other, not to her. This may include changing seating arrangements so certain family members sit nearer one another.

2. Estranged family members are asked to face each other with a table or chair between them and a pile of books or bricks at one side (see Fig. 15). They are told to build a wall in the area between them. Taking turns, each person places one "brick" in the wall at a time, explaining the particular barriers that "brick" represents that prevent him from talking to the other person. Once the wall is in place, the members in conflict are asked to choose which "bricks" they would like to work toward eliminating first. The brick they choose is then removed from the wall and discussed in terms of:

"How did this 'brick' come between us?"

"What keeps it there?"

"What can we do, individually and together, to get rid of it?" This exercise also can be used by family members who have difficulty trusting each other, with the wall labeled a "trust barrier."

3. The therapist asks estranged family members to send each other brief, taped messages each day in which they express their needs and feelings. The length of the tapes can be determined by the therapist and family members. The exercise should be used for a limited time and should help specific members begin to experience direct contact with one another without outside interference.

4. The therapist dramatizes the "go-between" position one member plays in the family as well as the kinds of "middleman" communication he observes. Seating is arranged so that the member who typically plays a go-between role is in the middle and family members whom he serves as mediator are on either side of him. Estranged family members are instructed to send messages, in their usual manner, through the go-between. As the exercise progresses and family's mounting discomfort and frustration become evident, the exercise is stopped and all are asked to discuss how they felt

Figure 15.   When family members fail to communicate directly with each other, it's often due to barriers that exist between members. An effective method of bringing these barriers to a family's awareness is through using "books" or other items to help them describe and visualize these blocks.

about the experience. Family members frequently state that they found it easier to stop talking to the other person rather than to talk through a third party. The go-between may also express considerable resentment and discomfort about being placed in the middle of most family differences and disagreements, although he or she may also enjoy the feeling of being indispensable that can come from this role. When these feelings have been shared, the family go-between may be removed and the estranged members asked to talk directly to each other with the therapist providing assistance as needed.

Problem / Family members attempt to control what other family members say, often to prevent the expression of negative feelings.

Interventions /

1. The therapist intervenes with a statement such as: "Let him speak for himself; we've agreed we won't interrupt each other."

2. The therapist identifies the "controlling" action that is taking place by pointing out the manner in which one member is trying to control or silence another member. The interactions that precipitated the "controlling" action are explored with the family. The member on the receiving end of the "controlling" incident should be encouraged to express her feelings about the experience. The controlling member should receive sensitive guidance from the therapist in helping him to understand why he reacted as he did and what other alternative behaviors might be open to him.

Problem / Family members use double-bind or contradictory communication with other members resulting in a "damned if I do and damned if I don't" position.

Interventions /

The therapist doubles for the person who receives these messages in an attempt to bring everyone's attention to the receiver's confused and conflicting feelings as to: (1) what the message really means and (2) what should be done about it.

GENERAL TECHNIQUES DESIGNED TO IMPROVE FAMILY COMMUNICATION

These techniques can be effective with all of the aforementioned problems.

Family Discussion Assignments / Family members are asked to meet together outside the therapy setting to talk during the week. (See Fig. 16.) The authors frequently suggest two sessions, limited to 45 minutes each, and have the family agree, before leaving the counseling session, on where and when the discussions will be held. Issues that might be discussed are suggested and the family is asked to tentatively agree on topics for discussion. However, the family's agenda should always be open to other issues that might spontane-

Figure 16.   Family meetings can be extremely beneficial in helping a family explore its interactional patterns. However, the therapist should caution family members from using these meetings as a forum to make their point to other members.

ously arise during the week. One family member is asked to serve as moderator, whose primary role is to stop arguments and be sure everyone has a chance to talk. Another member is asked to take notes on the discussions and bring them to the next therapy session. These roles should be rotated to provide everyone with an opportunity to experience family communication and interaction from a more objective position. The therapist may sit in on one family meeting and lead a post-session discussion of what took place.

Sometimes families report difficulty in discussing certain issues or in reaching mutually satisfying outcomes in their home discussions. The therapist may ask a family to discuss these issues in his presence, but without his participation, so both he and they may gain added insights into where breakdowns are occurring.

As the discussion progresses and areas of breakdown become apparent, the discussion is stopped and family members are asked how they are experiencing the discussion. They are asked to identify particularly frustrating points in the discussion that may have led to an eventual breakdown in communication, to identify any actions of their own that led to communication breakdowns, and to suggest ways in which they might be able to improve those actions. The therapist's observations on points of communication breakdown also are helpful when a family has not been able to discern these themselves.

The family is encouraged to continue with its discussion with the goal of developing more productive ways of interacting. This process may be repeated as often as necessary, with the family's discussion and the therapist's comments centering on points of breakdown as well as reinforcing interactional patterns that everyone found to be satisfying and productive.

Message Dissection / This model is patterned after some of Virginia Satir's early communication work and can be used when a pattern of communication breakdown consistently occurs between family members. The sender of a message is asked:
"What did you want?"
"What did you do?"
"What did you get?"
The receiver of the message then is asked:
"What did you hear?"
"What did you make of it?"
"What did you do?"
Regular use of this technique should produce understanding as to where and how communication is breaking down. If the receiver perceived the message correctly but did not act on it, the factors that kept him from doing so should be explored; these factors might include past anger or hurt or feeling blamed or controlled in the discussion.

Audio- or Videotape Playback / This involves asking families to listen to audio- or videotape playbacks of portions of a family session. In so doing family members may gain a better awareness of discrepant and destructive communication patterns they may be using unwittingly.

Breakdowns in Self-concept Reinforcement

Problem / Family members feel unloved and worthless because they are not receiving caring messages from other family members.

Interventions /

The therapist offers reinforcement and support of a family member's self-worth in the following ways.

1. The therapist forms coalitions with certain members, supporting their perceptions when appropriate. This should be done in a balanced manner with all family members receiving support from the therapist at different times, although forming exaggerated or very one-sided coalitions is sometimes used in order to accomplish specific goals such as eliminating destructive "status quo" patterns in a family system. Generally, this is a risky approach for the beginning therapist unless it is done under careful supervision.

2. The therapist uses the "positive double-bind." This concept, defined by Luthman and Kirschenbaum (1974), was discussed in Chapter 4. The positive double-bind stresses the good intentions of the members of the family while also pointing out approaches the group has tried that haven't worked well. Then family members, when asked to try new behaviors with a better chance of success, inevitably agree because they want to appear to be concerned and motivated to do something about the family's problems. With such an approach, it is hard to avoid growth and change, and an improved self-concept of all family members is a very frequent outcome.

Problem / Family members feel unloved and worthless because they negate caring messages sent them or refuse to hear them.

Interventions /

1. Asking family members to remember times when they felt other members cared for them and to reminisce about shared posi-

tive activities and feelings frequently points out that other members, in fact, care about them and have expressed this caring. Discussions may focus on enjoyable times the family has shared, such as holidays, birthdays, and anniversaries, as well as other positive spontaneous happenings. Discussion also may focus on times when the family remembers working together to achieve a common goal.

2. Family members are asked to write at least two compliments or things they like or admire about each other member and to place it in a box held by the person about whom it is written. Family members take turns drawing one compliment from their box, reading it, and giving their reaction to it. If they cannot accept a compliment, they are asked to return it to the person who wrote it and tell him why they can't. That member then is asked to react to the return of his compliment. Statements such as "That's what always happens at home," or "After awhile I stop trying to say anything nice," frequently are made. Receiving positive strokes can help build the self-concept of members. At the same time, individuals who are blocking other family members from sending them caring messages generally gain some awareness of why they receive so little reinforcement from the family.

Problem / Family members fail to send self-concept reinforcement messages or engage in a considerable amount of blaming, ignoring, or accusing behavior toward each other.

Interventions /

1. The therapist models positive reinforcement behavior by sharing her feelings and thoughts about the family. She also points out the common experiences and relationships the members share that link them together.

2. The therapist enforces ground rules that force people to stop attacking and blaming, to recognize individuality, and to find more constructive ways to express themselves.

3. The therapist checks out messages with family members who have a hard time conveying feelings to other members: Check with one member:

"How do you think Bill feels about you? Does he care?"

"How do you get this message?"

Then, with the second member:

"How does this fit in with your feelings about Mary?"

"Did you know she thought you saw her this way?"

"What *do* you like about Mary?"

"How did you let her know this?"

"Can you tell her about it now?"

The method can be reversed as necessary. The exercise emphasizes the importance of sending clear, caring messages to all family members.

4. The group is asked to chart audio- or videotaped playback sessions of its family interview. Each family member is given a chart similar to the one in Chapter 3 (Fig. 9, p. 45) and asked to pick another member to listen to and/or observe during a replay of the interview. Observers should use a plus sign (+) to indicate times that members receive a positive message. Completion of the charts by family members and compiling all the plus signs by the therapist into a single family chart can indicate the nature of communication within the family. The exercise also points out which members are receiving many negative messages and/or few positive messages.

5. The technique of having the family make "love lists" was devised by therapists from the American Institute of Family Relations. Though the technique is used primarily in marriage counseling, it can be adapted easily for use with families. Members are asked to make three lists, which should include the following information: ways in which each member feels loved by his family, different ways in which a family member would like to feel more cared for, and the means by which the family might send these messages. The family shares the various lists. Each family member picks one item from every other member's list that he or she will work on during the coming week. Further information on use of this technique is described in the book *The Marriage Savers* by Koch and Koch (1976).

6. The family performs the "needs and appreciation" exercise cited earlier in this chapter.

7. In the family in which members feel neglected because other members put the bulk of their time and energy into other activities and individuals, the therapist points out the possibilities for changing this pattern. The following exercises can be helpful.

Help each family member determine what time in their present schedules might be available to devote to the family. This can be done by asking each family member to make a schedule of typical weekly activities and then label each time block in one of the following ways:

Non-negotiable time. I need to be doing this when I am doing it.
Negotiable time. This time would definitely be available to spend with the family.
Possibly negotiable time. I do have other commitments at this time but would be willing to consider giving some of them up or rescheduling them in order to have time to spend with the family.

Once the lists are complete, the therapist helps the family mesh their negotiable time blocks and plan family togetherness time around them as the family feels necessary. In families where not enough jointly available negotiable time exists for such planning, the therapist helps the family bring their "possibly negotiable" available time blocks into the planning and utilize them as needed.

Help family members determine how they might enjoyably spend mutual time together. This exercise may be necessary with families who have had limited past experience in enjoying each other's time and company. Family members are asked individually to make lists of activities they personally enjoy doing or think they would like to try. If only a dyadal relationship is involved (e.g., the marriage), the two people can be asked to exchange lists and indicate three things on the other person's list that they would be willing to participate in. If the entire family is involved, the therapist can list all the activities mentioned by the family members on a blackboard or large sheet of paper, marking those activities mentioned by more than one family member accordingly. The family is then encouraged to discuss the possibilities open to them for enjoyable shared time from the lists, choose one or two activities they would like to start with, and make plans to implement these choices.

Problem / Family members have different styles of sending messages that show they care. This causes frequent "receiving breakdowns."

Interventions /

1. Family members describe how they learned particular styles of showing caring for one another. Family history material can aid in this discussion.

2. Two members with significantly different styles of expressing affection are asked to reverse roles. Each member spends at least

five minutes pretending he is the other person and expresses feelings he believes the person may have. The experience is discussed when participants return to their original roles.

Problem / Family members consistently tell other members how to do things or insist on doing things for them.

Interventions /

1. Divert the family member who is involved too much in other members' affairs into activities of his own. This allows the person less time and energy to devote to other members' activities. A married parent who is too involved with a child might redirect his or her energies into the marital relationship.

2. Support the efforts and intentions of an overinvolved member, but restructure the nature of the involvement. This technique is similar to the method of relabeling behavior and is especially appropriate when the overinvolved family member has resisted the idea of becoming less involved. At the same time, the overinvolved member may demonstrate some need to please the therapist and/or to appear helpful.

> The family consists of an overinvolved grandmother, her dependent, insecure daughter, and a grandson who exhibits behavioral and academic problems. The boy was manipulating his mother and grandmother, playing them against each other. A single, consistent authority in the boy's life was sorely needed. Everyone verbally agreed that the adult authority should be the boy's mother. It was decided that the grandmother should not be a surrogate parent but rather should serve as an ally and helper to the therapist. Recognizing the grandmother's importance in the family, the therapist noted that she must feel burdened with the responsibility of monitoring the boy's performance in school and settling problems that arose between the son and his mother at home. The grandmother agreed. The therapist said he felt it wasn't fair, since she had raised her family and deserved some time to herself. Her daughter agreed that she and her son would try to work

out their problems without calling on her mother for assistance. If they couldn't, the problems would be brought to the next therapy session. The therapist told the grandmother he would try not to bother her with these problems, though he recognized that she knew a great deal about the family and had helped them on many occasions in the past. He also told her he might occasionally need to call on her for help. She agreed to be available in emergencies. The grandmother was contacted on two occasions about family matters in which she was appropriately involved: the mother's arranging for her to babysit with a younger child and the boy's "runaway" excursions to the grandmother's when he and his mother had a fight.

3.   Intensify the overinvolvement of the family member to the point they feel "taken advantage of." This generally results in the member's eventual withdrawal from inappropriate involvement.

Eric's father tended to become too involved in his son's problems at school. The therapist took the father up on his complaint that "the school never lets me know what's going on." He talked with the vice-principal about the school calling the father, regardless of how minor a situation might seem, when there was concern about the son's behavior or a decision to be made involving the boy. The therapist told the vice-principal that he believed this might eventually alleviate the problem of the father's overinvolvement. Three weeks later, after receiving the seventh call in a week, the father told the vice-principal he did not want to be bothered with these matters any longer. He indicated his confidence that the school could work out its problems with his son without his involvement. The therapist supported the father in his decision at the next session. As the father's overinvolvement in Eric's school life decreased, the boy began to display more responsible behavior and raised his grades at school, knowing his father would no longer be willing to bail him out.

Expectations Family Members Hold for Each Other

Problem / Family members hold expectations for one another that deny members' individuality. Family members use expectations that they hold for other family members as measuring sticks by which to determine how much these members care about them.

Interventions /

All problems in member-to-member expectations are dealt with in basically the same way. The parties involved, especially the members who hold the expectations, must be made aware of expectations that are unrealistic and inappropriate. Members who hold unreasonable expectations should be helped to identify the source of their expectations and to see how they presently fit the people in the family. Family members frequently have problems in defining the expectations they hold for each other. If this is the case, the therapist can note and follow through on disappointments that family members express about one another. Invariably, this leads to the discovery of unfulfilled expectations.

Awareness of expectations can be facilitated by the therapist by discussion of these expectations with the family or by use of one of the following exercises:

1. Have family members do a "ten-year projection." Although it can be used with discrepant marital partner expectations, this technique is especially effective in working with a child who is not meeting parents' expectations. Family members whose expectations are not being met by another member are asked to imagine what they would like to see that person doing and what they hope his life will be like ten years in the future. Families that are especially responsive to action techniques can be asked to physically set up an imaginary scene, placing that person in the role they feel is best for him. The family should use available furnishings and other family members in the scene, as appropriate.

The person for whom the expectation is being held should be asked for his observations of the family's ten-year projection for him when the scene is complete. Differences of opinion in what the person wants for himself and what other members want for him are identified. The roots of the differing expectations are explored and an effort is made to work toward a mutually acceptable future projection for his life. This technique often reveals that family members' long-range goals and values are very similar. In these situations, the exercise can serve as a unifying experience for a family, since it reminds the group of values they hold in common.

2. Family members plan a room together. This technique is adapted from premarital counseling. It is especially effective in pointing out differing expectations that spouses hold for their life together. The technique also can be used to deal with parent–child relationships. A couple is asked to set up its "dream living room" in as much detail as possible, using available props to symbolize desired furnishings. Differing expectations of what the room should be like usually arise early in the exercise. The nature of these differing expectations, particularly if they extend into a couple's larger life and what can be done about the differences can be dealt with by answering these questions: (a) What is the source of your expectations? (b) How do the expectations fit your present life? (c) What are you going to do about the expectations that are not workable? A successful conclusion to the exercise comes when the two people are able to set up a living room that expresses their individuality while at the same time providing a place where they can live comfortably together.

3. Ask a family member to make a sculpture of his family as he would like it to be and to give each member a sentence to say that fits their position. The family "sculptor" should be the member who appears to have unrealistic expectations for one or more members. The sculpture will make the person's expectations more explicit. When the sculpture is completed, the therapist asks each family member to explain how he feels about the position and sentence assigned to him. Family members who disagree with their assigned roles and perceptions should be invited to discuss the expectations family members hold for one another, where those expectations originated, and how they presently are working. A successful conclusion to this experience might involve an especially sensitive family member doing a bonding, integrative sculpture of the family in which everyone feels comfortable.

Breakdowns in Handling Differences

Problem / Family members equate disagreement with "not caring."

Interventions /

Two family members who seem emotionally separated from each other because of this stereotype are invited to reverse their roles. Participants should become aware that unique personalities and experiences produce differing perceptions. They should learn that disagreement or differences of opinion are a natural outcome of differing perceptions and are not necessarily a deliberate attempt to hurt another person. Participants are asked to close their eyes and to imagine that they are the other person and are experiencing the situation from his perspective. Dialogue between therapist and participants is kept at a minimum as the therapist tries to help each person achieve some empathy for the other person's position. Finally, both people are asked to open their eyes. They are then given the last sentence spoken by the person whose role they have taken before the reversal began and asked to continue the conversation, still playing the other person's role. Participants should return to their original roles when the therapist notes that empathy for each other's position seems to be developing. The therapist opens discussion following the role reversal by asking both participants how they felt about the exercise.

Problem / Families use ineffectual tools for handling differences such as: (1) attack, (2) avoidance, or (3) surrender.

Interventions /

1.   Once the therapist has identified ineffective patterns for handling differences, she can discuss the patterns with each member, using this framework:

"What do you want from the people in the family?"

"What do you *do*?"

"What do you *get*?"

This approach should make a person aware of the ineffective way he handles differences with other people.

2.   Utilize audio- or videotapes of family sessions when differences arise in order to sensitize the group to ineffective patterns it may be using to deal with differences. Follow the procedure suggested above during or after the tape playing.

3.   When two family members seem trapped by unproductive ways of handling differences, Lederer and Jackson (1968) suggest the therapist should change roles with one member and model a more productive way of dealing with the differences facing the

family. The member with whom the therapist changes roles is given a chance to resume his role and continue the discussion with other family members as soon as he feels ready to do so.

4.   The therapist can use assignments to help family members experience more satisfying ways of dealing with their differences between sessions. A traditional assignment is to ask the family to try to use productive ways to resolve their differences — discussing the problems, sharing feelings, identifying areas of agreement, trying to negotiate with one member serving as moderator, utilizing compromise, and so on — during the week between sessions. If this type of assignment proves to be unsuccessful, a "small change" assignment is worth trying. The family is asked to make only a slight change in its usual unproductive way of dealing with differences. This can range from shifting the place where arguments tend to erupt to slightly altering everyone's usual role in a conflict. This technique is especially helpful for family members who consistently set such unreachable goals, involving major changes for themselves, that they become discouraged and blame themselves when they cannot reach their goals. The therapist can reassure these individuals that a smaller, attainable change not only may be adequate, but in fact may be preferable since it is more possible to maintain.

> The therapist asked one family to hold its arguments in the recreation room of the basement. Making a trip to the basement to fight quickly made the absurdity and uselessness of the new ritual apparent. The family soon reported that more problems were being worked out through discussion upstairs. If an argument was taken to the basement, disagreements were pursued with far less intensity and everyone seemed to have more understanding for another person's position.
>
> In another family, the therapist was able to secure an agreement from a very verbal, attacking family member to express herself in an argument only after all the others had had a chance to state their positions. By the time the silent member listened to what everyone else had to say, her anger usually had dissipated and her understanding of other people's positions had increased. Her comments began to reflect less anger and more understanding. Other family members responded by attacking her less and listening more.

5. Families that lack motivation or self-discipline to follow through on either traditional or "small change" assignments may be helped by an assignment technique known as the "therapeutic paradox" or "prescribing the symptom." Frequently, people refuse to admit that they have any control over their behavior in a difficult family situation, maintaining that they are "innocent victims." Someone else is always expected to make the first move in resolving differences.

With this technique the therapist assigns the group to "keep doing what you're doing, but do it better." This kind of assignment, to be successful, relies heavily on the therapist's credibility with the family and the relationship he has built. Obviously, a family may hesitate to carry out a request that seems to intensify its worst problem; therefore, the family usually agrees to carry out the assignment only to please the therapist or prove him wrong. Families may also be more willing to try this kind of assignment if they think they have tried other approaches to the problem that haven't worked and are stymied. The behavior they are asked to try in the assignment should not be in violation of the individuals' basic values or ethics.

An assignment may be introduced by the therapist in one of several ways:

> "I know this might not make much sense to you right now, but would you all agree to try something that might help?"
> "I need more information about your family situation before I can be of any help and I need your help in getting it." Reference to Herr and Weakland's *Counseling Elders and Their Families* (1979) would be helpful to the reader who decides to use this approach.
> "We frequently find in helping people make changes in their behavior that a problem has to get worse before it gets better, so perhaps it would be best to work on making that happen right now."
> "If it turns out that you can't get rid of this problem, you can at least practice being more in control of it by participating in this assignment."

These assignments should not be made unless a family has some respect for the therapist's competence and agrees to try them. Without this perspective, the therapist probably will be labeled incompetent at best, and the family will leave therapy. The approach, though seemingly illogical, forces family members into a no-win situation in their battle to hold on to their behavior. A family using its behavior to control or punish other people loses control of the situation when it finds itself continuing the behavior under a therapist's direction and being praised for following instructions. If the family disobeys the therapist's instruction, the price it pays is sacrificing the old behavior pattern and experiencing more satisfying ways of interacting with one another. A family that maintains that it has no control over its behavior or whose members contend that others must change before they can themselves suddenly finds itself unable to defend such statements. Obviously, if family members can consciously initiate and carry out destructive behavior as prescribed by the therapist, the family *does* have some control over its behavior. The therapist must then ask family members what is to keep them from doing the same thing with more constructive behavioral approaches to the situation.

The therapist must exercise a considerable amount of discretion in initiating assignments of this type. They must not be used if the therapist fears that they may have damaging effects on any family member. If, however, the family is being asked to keep doing what it has been doing (and will undoubtedly continue to do without some kind of intervention), and asked in such a way that a change in this pattern will be likely to occur, their usage seems justified.

> Sally nagged and Tom left, so the young couple rarely settled its differences when an argument arose. The therapist gave them the following assignment. During their next argument, the husband was to sit at the kitchen table where most disagreements occurred. The wife was to stand over him and tell him why she was right and he was wrong for at least 20 minutes. He was not to respond to her comments but, as soon as she finished he was to leave the house and not return for at least three hours. The couple had considerable misgivings, but agreed to carry out the assignment for a week. Four days later, they called the therapist and told her they did not want to continue the assignment. Instead, they would begin trying some of the techniques they had discussed in the session that might help them deal more successfully with their differences. With the exception of two minor lapses that they were able to deal with themselves, the couple did not return to their old pattern.

Unique Dysfunctional
Interactional Patterns

Problem / The family is caught in repetitive interactional patterns that cause people pain, repetitive interactional patterns that fail to solve problems but instead perpetuate or intensify them, or repetitive interactional patterns that conflict with each other.

Interventions /

These strategies are designed to facilitate conscious change of dysfunctional patterns by the family on the premise that awareness will lead to change.

1. One strategy is for the therapist to confront the family with the dysfunctional interactional pattern verbally, when it occurs in the session, or through playback for the family of video- or audio-taped family sessions where the interactional pattern occurs.

2. Another strategy is for the therapist to make the family aware of its destructive interactional patterns and give assignments designed to stop those patterns during the week. These assignments can take one of several forms. First, assignments can be formulated and initiated by the therapist. In this case the therapist should always check with family members before the session ends to be certain they understand what the assignment involves and answer any questions or objections they have. Everyone must agree to do the assignment or it probably won't be carried out. The therapist must also discuss obstacles that might occur either within or outside the family's control that might prevent the assignment from being completed. Many therapists address the question, "What could you do to blow it?" to each member. Asking the question labels nonparticipation or sabotage of the assignment as an intentional act. It should also be made clear that the family can check by phone with the therapist, or vice versa, as needed, to determine how things are going on an assignment during the week. Sometimes the therapist asks the family to call him before discontinuing the assignment if members cannot or do not want to continue.

A family must respect the therapist and believe he is capable of and committed to helping relieve its pain if any assignment is to succeed. Even when a family is not successful in carrying out an assignment, the experience provides the therapist with invaluable information about where and why breakdowns occurred.

Mr. and Mrs. Larson complained about the late hours 15-year-old Linda was keeping. The therapist asked the family to complete a trust-building assignment before returning for their next session. The family agreed to follow the therapist's suggestion of extending Linda's weekend curfew to 11:00 P.M. She, in turn, promised to abide by these hours and to call if she was ever unavoidably delayed. At the next session, Mr. Larson angrily reported Linda had stayed out until midnight Friday and Saturday nights and charged that his suspicions were correct — Linda could not be trusted. The therapist explored the situation further and found that Mrs. Larson had told Linda she could stay out until midnight on Friday because of a special school activity. Mr. Larson, not knowing this, returned home late Friday night from a business trip and was furious because Linda was not there. With this information, the focus of therapy shifted to the poor communication patterns between father and mother and the mother's tendency to act as "middleman" between father and daughter. Frequently, she attempted to interpret his wishes to the children in a manner she felt to be more reasonable but which often negated his meaning. Her arrangements with the children ("It's okay if you stay out a little later this weekend because of all the baby-sitting you did with your little brother this week") were never reported to the father.

A second form an assignment can take is for the therapist to ask, "What would you suggest if you were the therapist?" Assignments formulated by a family, with the therapist's assistance, are frequently more effective than those devised by the therapist acting alone. Family members first must be able to state how they contribute to and perpetuate a dysfunctional pattern and then they must identify the behavior they would like to see replace this pattern. Finally each member is asked:

"What could you do to make the desired behavior happen?"
"What parts of achieving this desired behavior would you be willing to work toward as a goal during this coming week?"
"How will you work toward reaching this goal?"
"What possible obstacles do you see in achieving the goal? How will you overcome them?"

Here is a simple example of how a family prescribed and carried out such an assignment.

> The family was spending virtually no enjoyable time together. Family members quickly realized they had a distant, essentially negative relationship. Each family member volunteered ways to change his present living schedule to allow more time to be with the family. The therapist helped family members mesh the times they would be available into two periods each week when everyone would be together. The task completed, the therapist helped them decide on the specific things they would do during these shared times.

A third form for an assignment designed to stop destructive interactional patterns is called "Let's pretend we have this rule." This exercise is designed to increase family members' awareness of a dysfunctional interactional pattern and to show what life might be like if they stopped following the pattern. Though the technique generally is used during a therapy session, sometimes it can be used as an assignment for a family to carry out during the week. Ask the family to follow a positive rule essentially opposite to what is being done. For example, parents in the Larson family, discussed previously, might have been asked to agree to follow this rule: "All major decisions affecting the children will be made jointly and transmitted to them by both of us."

Conversely, if this approach shows little promise of being successful, family members can be asked to follow a rule that intensifies and makes glaringly apparent the destructive interactional pattern. The Larson family might have been asked to try following this rule: "*All* of Father's wishes or instructions regarding the children are to be transmitted to them by Mother. Father will agree during this period not to tell any of the children directly anything he wants. He also agrees to transmit any displeasure he may feel through Mother."

The decision to make an assignment like this should be based on the therapist's assessment of the family's motivation and ability to carry it out. The therapist must decide whether learning possibilities outweigh potential problems before assigning a negative rule. Whether the assignment is used only in a session or at the family's home, the therapist should ask the members, at the beginning, what they think it will be like to follow the rule. They should be encouraged to discuss their experience with the rule when the assignment is completed. If they have been asked to experience only a negative rule, the therapist should get the family's idea about how this interactional pattern might be changed to make family life more satisfying for everyone.

ALTERING DYSFUNCTIONAL PATTERNS THROUGH INDIRECT MEANS

The direct approach mentioned earlier has its limitations and sometimes stronger medicine is needed. Families frequently persist in engaging in unproductive behavior that produces pain. These families may fear change or believe that certain members don't care and can't be trusted to change. At times, members cling to the reinforcements offered by their present behavior, such as attention or control. A family member's resistance to change may be observed through statements and behavior indicating that he or she views the situation from a narrow, rigid perspective that usually discounts his or her role in creating and sustaining the problem. Therapists who encounter families that have seen several other therapists with little success should be wary of spending much time on assignments that promote conscious change. One of the following indirect strategies may be helpful in dealing with this kind of family.

Reframing or relabeling behavior is a technique that was mentioned briefly under the section dealing with family communication problems. The therapist suggests a way for the family to look at and explain its problems from other than its current perspective. The new perspective must be compatible with the ways the family views life. New explanations for various kinds of behavior frequently make it impossible to continue those behavior patterns. It is frequently successful to relabel a family member's anger as concern; nagging may be relabeled as "trying to help." This relabeling allows the angry or nagging person to stop being a bad guy. Other family members begin to view him differently and everyone usually becomes more open to considering additional ways of dealing with the situation.

A successful use of relabeling follows.

Using relabeling with the Larson family, referred to earlier, the therapist redefined the mother's "middleman" activity as an effort to bring people in the family closer together. While the family considered the new definition, the therapist asked each member whether this was a goal he would like to work toward. Everyone agreed it was. They were asked if they would be willing to help Mother accomplish this goal. They agreed they would. They also agreed to seek ways in which the family might work together to accomplish the goal. Commitments to do these things were secured. After the session Mother's "middleman" activities decreased markedly.

Relabeling may be used negatively at times to bring about change, particularly when certain family members consistently and inappropriately attribute their behavior to unselfish motivations. Assuming a positive relationship exists with a family, the therapist might proceed in the manner described in the following example:

The wife was angry about her husband's habit of staying very late at parties they attended together. His behavior was most pronounced on nights preceding a week day. He insisted he had such a good time at parties that he just lost track of time. The therapist suggested that the husband might be punishing his wife because he didn't like the fact that she worked and knew she would be tired the day after she stayed up late at a party. The husband initially denied the therapist's interpretation, but later admitted his resentment about his wife's job and his feeling that she was neglecting the family. Through discussion and compromise, the therapist and the couple were able to move toward a better solution to the problem.

Relabeling or reframing behavior is described skillfully in the writings of the family therapists from the Mental Research Institute. The classic book *Change*, by Paul Watzlawick and his colleagues (1974), is especially recommended for a detailed development of this concept, as well as his more recent *Language of Change* (1978).

Restraining the family from improving is a technique used with families that are anticipated to be resistant or noncooperative. The family is confronted with the question, "Do we really want things to improve?" Haley (1977) suggests challenging the family to consider all of the other things that might get worse if a portion of its interactional pattern improved. The family might not come up with anything, in which case the therapist lists all of his concerns and again challenges the family as to whether it really wants to make the change it is considering.

Haley suggests that the therapist should begin by reassuring family members that he believes they would like to have a better life together. At the same time, he expresses his concern that changing the family's present behavior might not be the best way to accomplish the goal because unforeseen consequences might actually cause things to become worse. It is important that the last suggestion be unacceptable to the family in view of their perception of themselves. Hopefully, the family will be sufficiently provoked to prove it can make suggested changes without falling apart. As the family demonstrates that it can institute and maintain change, the therapist praises the members for dealing with their problems in a constructive manner.

> After several sessions, the therapist had failed to move members of the Brown Family away from their typical pattern of not speaking to each other when they were hurt or upset. She finally told them she was beginning to understand why they reacted in this manner when they were hurt. Everyone in the family appeared puzzled. The therapist said it was apparent that the family's members cared about each other and wanted to get along better, but that possibly being more open with their feelings and trying to work things out when concerns arose might not be the best way for them to do this. She supposed the family might need to be unhappy and feel isolated from each other from time to time so everyone would appreciate the times when things went well. She suggested that families who were happy most of the time might not really value those times as much as they would if they were unhappy some of the time. "Can you tell me how much of the time

all of you are happy together and how much of the time you're unhappy?" she asked. The family considered the question and generally agreed they were happy 30 percent of the time and unhappy 70 percent of the time. The therapist suggested that this happiness/unhappiness ratio might be the one with which the family was most comfortable. In fact, she noted, more "happy time" might lead to the family appreciating its good times less. "Maybe it's best to continue the way you are, keeping your hurts bottled up and not discussing them too much," she concluded. Several members angrily retorted that they could not only tolerate more happy times but would welcome them. They did not "need to experience so much time sitting in silence every week." At the next session, the family reported spending less time "sulking in silence" and more time in open discussion, using the techniques suggested to them in the sessions to solve problems. The therapist praised them, but suggested that their efforts probably represented a temporary improvement. Determined to prove her wrong, the family continued practicing open communication for three more weeks. Obviously happier with one another, the family was becoming skilled in solving a problem when it arose. The therapist praised the family for what they had accomplished and admitted that she had been wrong in her original supposition.

A family's resistance to change may be minimized by *asking the family to do something "a little differently"*; that is, to make a change so small that the family members would appear unreasonable if they refused. (See page 123.) As one piece of a family's interactional pattern is altered, it becomes impossible for them to maintain a former entrenched process and they find themselves developing new, more constructive ways for members to relate to one another.

A parent who consistently used verbal abuse to discipline his children was asked if he would refrain from this behavior half a day a week. He chose Thursday afternoon. At the next session he reported successful completion of his assignment and added that it seemed he had yelled far less at the children during the week. He reported everyone seemed to be getting along better. The assignment was repeated for another week with the father again reporting similar results.

Jeff consistently was blamed for most things that went wrong in the Lewis family. The therapist asked Jeff to do at least two things during the coming week that he knew would please his parents. He then asked the parents to see if they could identify those things and immediately express appreciation to Jeff. As anticipated, the parents began looking for Jeff's positive actions so they could report that they were tuned into the good things the boy did, as well as the bad. Their less critical attitude and Jeff's improved behavior were mutually reinforcing and everyone reported a much better week.

Asking the family to keep doing what it is doing but with greater intensity and skill, as described under the section on "Breakdowns in Handling Differences," can sometimes be helpful to a family's discontinuing a dysfunctional interactional pattern. Unlike the earlier assignment that asked a family to pretend it had a certain rule, this family need not be aware of what caused them to change. Families that are very resistant generally are not interested in receiving insights as to why they experience and demonstrate their resistance. Therefore, specifics of how the family changed its interactional pattern do not have to be discussed unless the family develops some awareness on its own of what happened and wants to discuss it with the therapist.

A mother complained of being depressed. She rarely got out of bed before noon because she couldn't bear to face the demands she felt her family placed on her. Housework wasn't done, meals weren't prepared, and jobs that couldn't be postponed had to be done by a 14-year-old daughter who was becoming increasingly resentful of her mother's behavior. The daughter and mother quarreled often. The mother said she was sick and could not help herself, a claim that prior medical and psychiatric attention did not substantiate. The father didn't know how to deal with the situation, and when the fighting started, he generally found a reason to leave. The mother was told to "keep doing what you're doing," and was assured that if she did not feel like getting up, that was her choice. Perhaps she needed even more rest than she was getting. The therapist instructed her not to get out of bed before 3 P.M. during the coming week, under any circumstance. Realizing this would intensify housework demands on the daughter, the therapist told the daughter to complain even more than previously, but only when her mother was in bed. She was instructed not to complain in her mother's room but in an adjoining room and loudly enough for her mother to hear. The father was asked to leave the house at once when his wife and daughter began arguing and not to return for a significant period of time. Somewhat skeptically, the family agreed to go along with the assignment. At the next session, the mother reported she had found it impossible to stay in bed later than 8 A.M. after carrying out the assignment for one day. She had got out of bed, done most of the housework, and prepared the family's lunch. The daughter said she and her mother had gotten along better during the week. The father said he had stayed home more, since it was pleasant to be there when everyone got along. The therapist mildly scolded the family for not continuing the assignment and asked them to try again the following week. They agreed, but returned the next week reporting similar results.

An excellent example of "prescribing the symptom" is found in the chapter on "Overt Intergenerational Conflicts" in Herr and Weakland's book, *Counseling Elders and Their Families* (1979).

Improving Family Climate

Simply stated, the desired goal of family therapy is for family members to feel better about living and interacting together. The family climate ("what it feels like to be in this family") is the product of the interplay of the functional and/or dysfunctional interactional patterns of the family. The techniques in this section should help move a troubled family toward more constructive interaction and an improved family climate, point out the pain that results from a family's present relationship, and reveal the positive feelings it is possible to experience from more constructive interactions. The techniques also help family members understand how other members feel about family interactional patterns. Hopefully, the "experiencing and understanding" they provide can be motivational factors that move a family toward change.

These techniques generally include two basic types of intervention. In the first type the therapist shares the feelings he is presently experiencing with the family and asks if anyone else has similar feelings. Family members who express similar feelings are helped to identify the interactional process that might have prompted those feelings. A classic example of the successful use of such an intervention came from Virginia Satir, who told of experiencing a stomachache in a session with a very difficult family. Reaching in her purse to get some antacid tablets, she spontaneously offered the roll of tablets to the family. Every member took one, and the matter of how this family felt in interaction with one another was successfully broached.

The therapist then goes on to help members identify other times in the family's daily interaction when these feelings occur and helps them focus on the dynamics of those interactions. Sometimes a family member persists in denying his negative feelings. The therapist, attempting to move the person toward greater self-awareness, acknowledges his lack of negative feelings, but also notes that the individual must feel "reasonably comfortable with things the way they are." The member is then asked to share with the family what is happening right now that makes him feel comfortable. Only the most frightened, rigid individual will continue to deny his negative feelings in such a situation, particularly when other family members are admitting and giving evidence of their pain.

With the second type of intervention the therapist, observing tension or discomfort in the family, asks family members, "What is your body saying to you right now?" This can help members consistently experience tension or pain in a part of their bodies, such as their stomachs or heads. The therapist can help those people become aware of the origin of those feelings by using a modification of the "empty chair" technique, described in an earlier chapter. The therapist places an empty chair across from the troubled family member and asks him to imagine that the affected part of his body is sitting there. He then asks the person to sit in the chair and try to speak for his hurting part, addressing such issues as "What am I feeling right now?" and "What does this part want to say to the rest of my body?" Comments can focus on *when* the part of the body feels discomfort and what the part feels its "total person" could do to help it feel better. After these issues have been addressed, the family member is asked to return to his original chair and become a total person. He is asked to respond to what the body part told him about its pain. This exercise also can be helpful in making other family members aware of how a certain member experiences the family's climate.

A Concluding Example

The following case example illustrates the use of some of the techniques discussed in this chapter.

The Roherke family was concerned about the behavior of the two oldest boys. Mr. Roherke, 46, had married Mrs. Roherke, 38, two years earlier. He was not the natural father of the three children, Cal, 17, Rod, 14, and Linda, 12. The children had virtually no contact with their natural father, who lived on the West Coast, had remarried, and sent them only an occasional card or gift. Cal had returned to the family six months earlier after spending nearly a year in a correctional facility. He resented his stepfather, attended an "alternative" high school in the community, and spent long periods of time away from home. Rod, a ninth grader, was barely passing. Although he shared some mechanical interests with his stepfather, he frequently got into arguments at home with both parents because of his grades, choice of friends, and "bad attitude." The family reported no problems with Linda, who was in sixth grade.

Therapy Goal 1 / Improve communication in the Roherke family, especially between the stepfather and the two boys.

Dysfunctional interactions noted during the therapy session included dad "preaching" at the boys and not listening to them; the boys becoming increasingly withdrawn and expressing their resentment by "dirty looks"; and mother's "middleman" efforts to prevent a fight between her husband and the boys.

Interventions /

1.   The therapist used "listening feedback" techniques, particularly in interchanges between the stepfather and the boys.
2.   The therapist used "doubling" for the boys, especially Cal, to help bring out unexpressed feelings.
3.   The therapist pointed out "nonverbal" messages the boys were sending and exploring their meaning.
4.   The therapist constructed a symbolic "wall" between the stepfather and Cal and explored ways in which it might be removed.
5.   The therapist dramatized the mother's "middleman" role in one session by placing her between her husband and the boys and routing their communication through her.
6.   The therapist rearranged chairs so that the stepfather and the boys could talk directly to each other.
7.   The therapist assigned family discussion sessions at home. This assignment initially failed and family members needed further practice with this kind of communication in the session before they were able to succeed with it on their own.

Therapy Goal 2 / Modify the parents' unrealistic expectations for the boys.

Mr. and Mrs. Roherke tended to focus on high grades and attending college, and gave little consideration to the boys' own interests and inclinations.

Interventions /

1.   The therapist's initial discussion focused on the source of these expectations. The father's expectations stemmed from his feelings of inadequacy about himself and his work. He believed successful people were "educated" and held "white collar" positions. The therapist recognized the father's good intentions in wanting the boys to have something better than he had.

2. The therapist asked Mr. and Mrs. Roherke to do a ten-year projection for the boys. This resulted in the expression of a number of shared values apart from occupation.

Therapy Goal 3 / Eliminate a dysfunctional family interactional process or rule.

A family argument usually occurred after church on Sunday, which the parents attended regularly, but the boys seldom. Angered at seeing the boys lying around in their pajamas on returning home, the parents criticized the boys for their laziness, their nonattendance at church, and whatever else came to mind. These angry accusations usually caused the boys to leave the house for the rest of the day.

Interventions /

1. The therapist utilized a "small change" assignment. The family was asked to build an "unhappiness expression" time into Sunday morning, right after breakfast. This would give everyone a chance to air complaints about everyone else early in the day. Members who wished to go to church would do so. While in church, they might wish to reflect further on the family discussion and any wrongs they had committed against each other during the week. As hoped for, resentments expressed at the morning meeting were done in a less hostile, less attacking manner than previously. The family subsequently experienced a relative "gripe free" Sunday three weeks in a row. They were also able to share an enjoyable activity, planned during their morning discussion time. The next week, they asked to discontinue the Sunday "unhappiness expression time."

7
DISRUPTIONS IN THE THERAPEUTIC PROCESS

Therapy Never Seems to Get Started

Fred and Grace Mattson were referred for family therapy by a local attorney who was a friend of the family. Seemingly open and cooperative, they expressed concern about a 16-year-old daughter who had been arrested twice for shoplifting. They were worried about the effect her behavior might have on the family's younger children. They appeared willing to consider the possibility that the girl's behavior might be influenced by problems in the family's relationship and agreed to a second interview involving the whole family. At the second session, everyone cooperated, though the therapist observed the difficulty the parents and the 16-year-old daughter were having in talking openly with one another. The family readily agreed to a third session. Three days before the next session, Mrs. Mattson canceled the appointment. She made it clear that the family did not wish to continue with therapy.

Invariably, the therapist in such a situation asks himself, "What went wrong?" The apparent success of the previous session had left him looking forward to seeing the family again. When the next session is canceled and the family leaves therapy, the therapist must objectively consider both external and internal factors that might have influenced the family in deciding to terminate.

External factors could include obstacles such as illness, job problems, or financial difficulties. While taking these into consideration, the wise family therapist also examines the internal aspects of a therapy experience. The therapist reviews the family's earlier therapy sessions with an eye toward answering the following questions:

1.   Did a clear picture of the family's expectations of therapy emerge? Did the therapist remember to explain clearly what would be involved in the therapy sessions? Did he spell out what the family would be expected to accomplish? Did he clearly define his role or was the family allowed to look on him as a miracle worker who could wave a magic wand and make everything better? Did certain family members expect the therapist to pronounce judgment on a family "culprit" and dictate who should make specific changes in the behavior and why?

2.   Were the family's previous therapy experiences and their results fully explored? Did the therapist provide an opportunity for family members to discuss previous unproductive therapy experiences in order to determine whether old disappointments and fears might negatively affect their attitudes and willingness to participate now?

3.   Did every family member mutually decide which goals to work toward, or did the therapist dictate the direction the sessions were to take? Did the therapist focus on marital problems that he perceived as destroying the family when, in fact, the group itself remained convinced the main problems lay in the behavior of a child? Was every family member committed to the idea that this was a family problem, or did most members continue to see the problem as the sole responsibility of one member?

4.   Specifically, what might have happened in the therapy sessions that might have threatened or frightened some family members? Might one member have felt he was being portrayed as a villain or bad guy? Might one member who played a "middleman" role have feared that as the family became close he might be left out? Were too many feelings coming out too fast? (See Fig. 17.) Moving too fast can be especially threatening to families that previously bottled up their anger or perceived disagreements or the expression of differences as meaning that certain family members didn't care about other family members. A family that previously restrained its emotions might consider itself to be in a state of collapse when one or more of its members suddenly pour out their feelings.

Frank Pittman (1978), at a meeting of the American Orthopsychiatric Association, said people most often leave therapy because too much change is happening too fast. When families attack a ther-

Figure 17.   When breakdowns in the therapeutic process occur with families, it's important for the therapist to review what has occurred in the therapy sessions. Often, too many feelings come out too fast, creating an overwhelmed feeling in one or more family members.

apist's competence or the validity of the therapy sessions, they may actually be expressing discomfort about the therapist expecting too much to happen too soon.

On the other hand, the therapist who keeps sessions so tightly structured that family members are unable to freely express their feelings is asking for trouble. Ground rules that stifle necessary expression of feelings quickly become counterproductive. People must have an opportunity to discuss how they feel about what is happening to them within the family. Discussion must take place in a way that offers a family member a release valve without becoming destructive to other family members.

Therapy Goes Well and Then Seems to Founder

John and Laura Watts and their daughters Linda, 15, and Darlene, 12, are at their fourth therapy session. The family sought help initially because Linda was experimenting with drugs, was achieving poorly in school, and had friends whom her parents considered to be unacceptable. The parents could not agree on how to deal with Linda's misbehavior. Darlene, reacting to increasing conflict in the home, was spending more time at a friend's. Initially, the family did well in therapy. Parents and children seemed to care about each other, appeared motivated to work on their problems, and readily accepted the way the therapist redefined their concerns about Linda. The parents agreed to work more closely together in dealing with the children and to begin attending a local parenting class. The family agreed to begin regular family discussions at home. Linda kept her curfew for a week and helped more at home and, by the third session, everyone reported a happier family relationship.

The family came to the fourth session appearing tense and angry. Linda, the father reported tersely, had stayed out all Friday night and didn't come in until early Saturday morning. John and Laura had a terrible argument when Linda came home. Laura thought her husband's punishment—grounding Linda for six weeks—was too harsh. She refused to speak to her husband for the rest of the weekend. Darlene went to her girlfriend's home after the parents' fight and refused to return home.

The therapist faces the danger of finding himself immobilized by the apparent hopelessness that seems to have gripped the Watts family. He faces two possibilities in regard to the family's blow up: (1) the family may terminate therapy, or (2) the disruption may prove to be a valuable learning experience for both the family and the therapist. Interventions that might help move the family toward the latter outcome include advance preparation for probable setbacks and dealing with breakdowns after the fact.

Advance preparation for probable setbacks was discussed in the chapter "Beginning Family Therapy." Additional work in this area might have been done with the Watts family *after* it began reporting positive changes in relationships. Questions initiating this type of discussion could have centered on how the family felt it would react if parental conflict arose over matters of discipline or if Linda began misbehaving again. The therapist also could have helped the family identify coping techniques that it knows didn't work in the past as well as what each member believes he or she might do to deal constructively with a future breakdown. Each member's responsibility to assure the family's positive movement could be stressed by asking what they might do to make things go back to their former negative state.

Breakdowns can be dealt with after the fact in the following ways:

1.   Take time at the beginning of the session to let everyone express frustrations and disappointments about what has happened. Without blocking expressions of feelings, try to keep the family from reverting to old, unproductive communication patterns (blaming, attacking, mind-reading, speaking for others, etc.) by stressing that these things have never worked for the family in the past and can only make matters worse.

2.   Help the family reconstruct, as logically and calmly as possible, the events that led to the breakdown. The therapist generally finds that family members have misinterpreted the actions of other family members. They frequently believe, inaccurately, that other members have deliberately done things to hurt them, and acting on this misperception, they retaliate by trying to "hurt" the person they perceive as the culprit. Delving into the reasons behind the Watts family's blowup, the therapist learned that Linda had interpreted her mother's depressed mood and sarcastic comments on Thursday night as being directed at her. Linda expressed herself this way: "No matter how hard I try, Mom's not going to be pleased, so why should I bother." In reality, Laura's disappointment had come from what she believed to be an unsuccessful job interview earlier in the day. When she returned home with a severe headache, Laura didn't share these concerns with her daughters, though she did discuss them with John later in the evening.

3.   Help family members to look at alternative ways that might have been used to deal more successfully with the problem. This provides ideas for coping with similar problems if they occur again.

4.   Identify and reinforce any positive steps the family took to deal with the situation. These could include *not* reverting to past destructive behavior patterns, a commitment to return to therapy to discuss the situation logically, members acknowledging some responsibility for their part in the problem, and efforts to seek, together, better ways of dealing with a given situation. Strengths the family has demonstrated in the past in understanding each other and coping with problems also can be identified and supported by the therapist.

5.   Again review with the family possible breakdowns in its relationship during the coming week. Ask members to pinpoint their possible responsibilities for potential problems, including what they might do to cause a breakdown to occur. If a breakdown did occur, what actions might they take to move the situation toward a positive outcome?

Setbacks are a part of every family's functioning. In fact, just as a baby must stumble a few times before he can stand alone, a family must encounter and cope with setbacks before it can grow. The best laid plans are those that prepare the family members for both the joys and the pains of the future. This does not imply that when things are going well the therapist should tensely await the inevitable bad days. Instead, it is intended to alert both therapist and family to the fact that setbacks happen and can, with effort and caring, be surmounted.

8

ENDING THERAPY

Each therapy session is an integral part of the entire therapeutic process. Therefore, the therapist must prepare to appropriately end individual sessions as much as he prepares to complete therapy with a given family. Therapy sessions generally end at a time previously understood by all participants. Enough time prior to that time must be allowed to review and recap the session.

During this time the therapist may have to be more directive to facilitate a constructive integration of the session. This is particularly important in concluding sessions in which family members have shown considerable emotional involvement and feeling. The family needs to begin thinking about what has happened as well as "feeling" its experience (Fig. 18).

Laura Dodson (1977) states, "It is a time to move from the emotional level to an intellectual level." Intellectualizing a family's emotional experiences is imperative for the family's growth and learning.

Session ending should include a discussion of how each family member felt during the session and how they feel about the experience as the session draws to a close. The therapist should review any assignments the family has agreed to and be certain that they are clear and that everyone is committed to completing them.

The ending of therapy itself is best done by mutual agreement between the family and the therapist. Unfortunately, mutual agreement isn't always possible. Family members may get angry and not return, possibly leaving the therapeutic task hanging in midair. Sometimes unavoidable events — illness, moving away, death — end therapy abruptly. Ideally, therapy ends either when a family's goals have been achieved or when the family has developed the coping skills and commitment to reach goals on its own. Though family interactional patterns may not completely meet a family's ideals, the patterns should be seen as being more workable and satisfying than in the past. Family members also should share a realistic expectation of future growth in their relationships. The family needs to accept the probability of future setbacks and disappointments in

Figure 18.   When ending family therapy sessions, the therapist generally will facilitate a constructive integration of what has transpired during the session. The family needs to move from the "gut" or feeling level to the "head" or thinking level of experience.

their life together; for Rome was not built in a day and utopia exists only in the minds of men. An acceptance of these principles and a willingness to face life's struggles and disappointments, as well as its joys and rewards, can indicate significant maturation and growth on the part of the family.

Therapy sometimes ends by mutual agreement, but neither the therapist nor the family feels satisfied because of the accomplishment of defined goals. Certain family members may have been unwilling or unable to risk the commitment and involvement needed to successfully solve mutual problems and to achieve closer relationships. For reasons beyond a therapist's control, a family may not have been able to relate to or work well with him or her.

Whatever the reason, the therapist's perception that little is being accomplished in therapy should be shared with the family. The group's perception of what has occurred during the sessions also should be solicited, along with the reasons they believe progress is not being made. Finally, the question of whether the family can productively continue in therapy should be answered by the therapist and the family. Situations and feelings change, and the door should remain open for a family's return at a future time if it wishes to do so.

The appropriate time to end therapy may be raised by either the therapist or a family member. Discussion of this possibility should include:

1.   Reiterating goals the therapist and family mutually agreed to work toward.
2.   Looking at what has happened during therapy to move the family toward achieving those goals, with special emphasis placed on the contribution individual family members believe they have made toward family growth.
3.   Asking family members if they presently feel ready to "try it on their own."

When a mutual agreement is reached to end therapy, the therapist again should emphasize the importance of everyone working together to maintain the family's present positive interactions. Therapists from the Ackerman Institute ask family members, "What could *you* do to make things in the family go back to where they were when you first came in?"

Therapy for some families is best concluded by scheduling final sessions less frequently. Occasional follow-up sessions may be suggested to the family, if the therapist believes they are necessary. Sometimes the decision for follow-up sessions is left with the family. Each member is asked how he might know if the family needs to return to therapy. The therapist may ask the family members to agree to sit down with each other if things come to that point, share their concerns with other family members, and arrive at a mutual decision about seeking further therapy.

Reviewing the family interactions detailed in the third chapter, the therapist can feel comfortable in terminating a family in therapy when he sees the following processes occurring in the group's interactions.

COMMUNICATION

- People say what they *think* and *feel* to each other, verbally and nonverbally.
- People check out the meanings of each other's statements if they don't understand.
- Family members talk directly to one another in a session, look at

one another while doing so, and are able to listen to and hear what each person has to say.
- Family members tell the therapist they are communicating better with each other when not in sessions.
- Family members no longer try to read each other's minds, talk for each other, or verbally place each other in no-win positions.

SELF-CONCEPT REINFORCEMENT

- Family members are able to give each other verbal and nonverbal reinforcement and support.
- Family members report feeling loved and cared for by other members.
- No one places blame for the family's problems.
- Family members assume responsibility for their own actions.
- Family members report and demonstrate meaningful involvements with each other.

HANDLING DIFFERENCES

- Family members resolve differences in constructive ways, by no longer attacking anyone who doesn't agree with them and by not avoiding or withdrawing from dealing with genuine differences of perception and opinion within the family.
- Family members are able to accept opinions and ideas that might differ from their own without looking on those differences as personal attacks, by being able to listen to and consider ideas and perceptions different from their own, by being able to yield or compromise when this type of effort appears to offer the most workable solution, and by being able to accept growth and change in other family members, which may involve those members introducing new ideas and perceptions into the family system.

MEMBER EXPECTATIONS

- Family members are willing to allow other people in the family to be individuals and to express themselves and experience life in their unique ways, assuming that their expression of individuality is not destructive to a mutually satisfying family relationship.

UNIQUE DYSFUNCTIONAL
INTERACTIONAL PROCESSES (DIPS)

- Destructive, pain-producing family DIPS, or rules, that have been identified in therapy are no longer present.

FAMILY CLIMATE

- *The therapist* feels comfortable being with the family and is not aware of any emotionally induced physical pains and/or tensions in their presence.
- *The family* reports "feeling good."

The therapist should begin preparing the family for the end of therapy in the beginning session. He remains aware throughout the therapy experience of the need to encourage the family's independent growth. Though the therapist initially may have to be more active and directive in the sessions, he should seize every opportunity to remove himself from the family's interaction.

In essence, the therapist's preparations for ending therapy are preparations for the family's beginning to learn how to cope with their problems as a cohesive, caring unit.

9
THE FAMILY THERAPIST

Use of Self

For all that is I
Is but a part of you.
Through you I experience
Small — yet large moments of self
Only to be understood
Through your gift of self.

The therapist quietly watched as the family struggled to free itself from its painful interactions. Years of pent-up anger and disillusionment had built a wall of distrust between the family's members. The therapist felt overwhelmed by the family's interactions as the session progressed. He suggested that everyone take a short break, primarily to allow time for him to gather his thoughts on what he might do next. He went to the bathroom and splashed cold water on his face. As he reached for a towel, he hesitated and looked at his reflection in the mirror. Etched on his face was the frustration, the pain, and the fear of being unable to help the family. He recalled watching an elderly woman and some children in the park a few days earlier. One child, who was alone, went to the old woman, who asked if something was wrong. "I have no one to play with," the child responded. The woman fumbled through her purse, pulled out a small mirror, and gave it to the child. She told him to look into the mirror. Although confused, the child complied. The elderly woman then said, "In that mirror is someone who was with you yesterday, is with you today, and will be with you tomorrow." The child, still confused, replied, "But it's me; I'm in the mirror." The woman smiled and responded, "Yes, it is you and no matter where, when, or what happens the person in the mirror will always be with you."

The therapist's thought returned to his image in the mirror. He smiled as he realized the image before him showed him a way to help the troubled family. He realized that he must openly share his feelings about the family's pain. The family, knowing his honest feelings, might be able to begin breaking through its wall of hurt and distrust. Most important, the therapist realized that he possessed the most effective tool available . . . himself.

Families that are not aware of what they are feeling frequently are unable to take the first important steps toward change. In therapy a variety of techniques are taught to promote an awareness of feelings among family members. However, techniques are no better than a therapist's skill in using them. The therapist's awareness of who he is and how he can utilize his own feelings and experiences in therapy can help break the chains that encircle a family in dysfunctional interactions. Imperfect though it might be, the most important tool in the therapeutic relationship is what the therapist sees, hears, feels, and ultimately does.

Family therapists must be concerned with making people aware of their fears, disappointments, hopes, and joys, and also with the way a family interacts to produce those feelings. Many of the exercises previously discussed, including audio- and videotaped feedback, can be used to make family members more aware of interactional processes and their role in sustaining them. The therapist will find, however, that mirroring those processes back to the family by sharing his own feelings and reactions to what appears to be happening can have considerable impact.

Luthman and Kirschenbaum (1974) point out in *The Dynamic Family* that when all else fails, a therapist's ability to share his feelings and reactions is the best way to move a family toward positive change. The therapist should not share his feelings and emotions to satisfy his own needs, but rather to improve each family member's ability to understand and relate to other members effectively.

The therapist should tell the family exactly what he sees happening in the session. Generally, it is best to stop after sharing these observations and to encourage the family to interpret what may be causing these behaviors or interactions. The therapist might note that "Mom and Dad seem to be having a hard time looking at each other today," or "Tom doesn't seem to be very comfortable with the conversation between his dad and sister."

The therapist should tap into his own internal feelings. He should ask himself whether he is experiencing anger, tension, or relief. Is it possible that the family is feeling, but not expressing, these same powerful emotions? The therapist's feelings frequently are felt by various family members. They usually feel relieved because someone outside the family circle has shared his emotions and freed them to discuss their feelings. When strong feelings occur as a result of direct interactions among family members, the therapist may have to explore the causes behind those feelings, in addition to exposing the feelings themselves. The therapist might say, "I sense the anger both of you feel over what happened last night," or "I feel extremely relieved that you shared that information with your mother."

The extent to which a therapist should reveal who he is, what experiences he has had, and how those experiences affected him remains a controversial issue (see Fig. 19). For the most part a family member's direct questions about a therapist's innermost feelings should be answered as honestly as possible. Although a therapist's attention is focused on helping family members improve their inter-

Figure 19.   The extent to which a therapist reveals himself is a debated issue. Although the therapist focuses on the family's issues, the therapeutic relationship should be a give-and-take one and may include some sharing by the therapist.

actions with each other, the therapy relationship should be a give-and-take situation, which may include some discussion about a therapist and his family. When is it appropriate for a therapist to share his feelings? The following material may help alert the therapist to situations when it is most appropriate:

1. A family member might be helped to become aware of something similar to what the therapist describes that is causing problems. The therapist might recall a time when he felt resentment and discomfort toward another person but chose to stifle rather than openly express his feelings and work toward their resolution, with ultimately dire consequences for the relationship.

2. Family members can be helped to learn how someone else handled a similar situation, and alternatives they had not considered may be introduced. The therapist might remember some problems he experienced with a child during a particularly difficult school year and how certain special community resources provided the encouragement and perspective needed to deal constructively with the problem.

3. The family may gain the realization that in spite of the frustration and difficulty they are experiencing now, survival and growth are possible. The pain, frustration, and failure a single parent has experienced following a divorce might be acknowledged with empathy by a therapist who had to cope with a similar situation.

4. Family members can be made to see that the apparent hopelessness of their experience can be surmounted. The therapist may have experienced a similar family crisis — terminal illness in the family or the sudden death of a family member — noting that though the experience was painful, his family lived through it and continued to function.

Caution should be exercised when sharing personal experiences with a family, especially when

1. The shared experience may force inappropriate solutions on a family and block a necessary and potentially constructive search for answers. Telling a mother how much better the therapist's life has been since she became more assertive in her marriage and encouraging the woman to do the same may offer an inappropriate,

potentially destructive solution to the family's problem. A more constructive approach might involve encouraging her and her husband to explore their relationship and the things each might be doing to contribute to the strains and disappointments they are experiencing.

2. The experience may block family members from exploring certain feelings that must be expressed and dealt with before they can move on to consider solutions. A therapist's sharing how he dealt with an aging, interfering, "live-in" parent and arrived at the "perfect solution" will be less than helpful to a family that first must work through their resentment toward the parent and the accompanying guilt before alternative ways can be considered to deal with the problem.

3. A therapist's sharing of personal experiences is borne out of anxiety with the family's situation and his need to quickly resolve the group's dilemma and move on. The therapist might minimize a family's financial pressures by jokingly referring to his own money problems: "It seems like I'm always coming up a little short." Seriously helping the family to realistically examine its financial resources might confront the therapist with some concerns about his own financial situation that he has been trying to avoid.

As a therapist shares his observations, feelings, or experiences, he constantly should check with the family to see whether what he is experiencing or has experienced fits them. The therapist should be alert to the family's nonverbal responses to the information he shares about his experiences. The therapist's feelings and emotions can be his most valuable allies in therapy, but there may be times when they do not accurately mirror a family's situation. These times are most likely to occur when

1. The therapist doesn't know the family very well. Until the therapist has a solid feeling for a family and its interactional patterns, sharing of personal experiences is inappropriate. Such sharing probably will come more out of the therapist's own past experiences than out of his feeling for what the family is experiencing.

2. The therapist finds himself experiencing the family's pain too intensely. The therapist may find himself feeling lost or confused with a family and might seriously question his ability to be of much help. He may experience a great deal of resentment toward a certain family member whom he is convinced will either severely limit

or block any positive change within the family. Frequently, unusually strong feelings a therapist experiences with a particular family come from earlier experiences with his own family. The effects of those experiences may fester and remain unresolved in the therapist's own life and are vividly experienced again when he comes in contact with a similar situation in another family.

Eva Leveton (1976) talks about the family "rescuer" role as being one that many family therapists have played in their families of origin. As a child, the therapist may have developed skill in protecting people from being confronted with painful feelings and issues. He may have concentrated on trying to keep everything running smoothly. The therapist who brings "rescuing" tendencies to a session with a family can effectively block the group's growth and change by protecting members and keeping them dependent on him at a time when they need to move toward independence and constructive control of their lives. Rescuing can emotionally isolate the therapist, who feels he must be in control of the situation to ensure that no one is hurt and as a result is not free to experience and share his own feelings and emotions with the family. A therapist who brings his unfinished personal business into a family session finds his perceptions blurred and his ability to provide meaningful help reduced.

The authors knew a therapist who wasn't very successful in working with families. The fathers in the families generally stopped attending after a couple of sessions. Examining her interactions with the fathers, they found that she consistently was confronting them too strongly and had a tendency to side against them with the mother or children. Exploring the situation more closely with a supervisor, they found many unresolved feelings from her own childhood experiences with a deserting father and an alcoholic, abusing stepfather frequently were reactivated in her work with families. She often perceived men as being the primary cause of a family's problem. She looked on them as being insensitive and uncaring in the same way she had perceived her father as a child.

The Faces of Therapy

Families have different needs at different times in therapy. Meeting the various needs requires the therapist to wear many different faces to help move families toward change.

Laura Dodson (1977) referred to the "other eyes, other ears, other senses" role of the family therapist. She discussed the need for the therapist "to provide an additional perception of the family, one which can help the family see more clearly what is happening in their personal system." Luthman and Kirschenbaum (1974) discuss the role from the standpoint of a therapist operating as a "camera," capturing data from the family and sharing his picture with the family members. These are nondirective roles in which the therapist acts primarily as an observer.

The therapist often finds himself wearing the face of a *facilitator* or *activator*. This position permits the therapist to provide the family with the security and safety to delve into its painful interactions. The therapist may set rules to ensure a free and safe flow of communication. At other times the therapist may physically place himself or other members of the family in positions to encourage or discourage certain interactions. The person in this role becomes the catalyst, the springboard for healthy interaction among family members. He responds to both nonverbal and verbal messages and uses the messages to move the family. The therapist never takes over for a family; rather, he gently moves, directs, and sets free its interactions. Though all of the faces a therapist assumes are, by nature, facilitative, it often is necessary for him to become more overtly directive and controlling.

The therapist at times puts on the expert's face and assumes the role of *educator*. Therapists who assume the expert's role must avoid the temptation to become a "god" since "gods" have no room for human error. Families must perceive some expertise in their therapists if they are to have their fears of therapy reduced and have a degree of confidence in his teaching.

Virginia Satir says, "Families come to the therapist because he is an expert, so he must accept the label and be comfortable in his role." The cloak of expertise should, however, be worn by the family therapist as a loose-fitting garment, to be donned when needed and removed when it proves to be unnecessary or counterproductive.

As a teacher, the therapist prepares his lesson plan from information provided by the family, not from what he suspects the family needs to know. The data received from family members is the text and the sharing of this information must be coordinated when the family is ready and able to learn.

Invariably, the therapist finds himself serving as a *model* for the family. This generally occurs in two ways. First, the therapist often uses himself to mirror what he sees occurring in the family. He may use overt physical or verbal behavior such as raising his voice or distorting his face to help family members see themselves through his actions. As a "reflection in a mirror," the therapist tries to be as exact as possible in modeling the family's interactions. Unlike his roles as a "camera," in this case he becomes the "picture" for the family. Second, the therapist models new ways of interacting or coping with difficult situations. For example, a male and female co-therapist team can demonstrate effective ways to resolve differences for a husband and wife by openly discussing a difference they may be experiencing at a particular moment in therapy. By sharing their disagreement and subsequent handling of their differences, the therapists allow the family to experience new behavior, following their model.

Laura Dodson (1977) suggests another role a therapist may play in dealing with family crises. She refers to the role as the "Bandaid or Truant Officer." Family members at times are submerged in pain due to unforeseen circumstances such as death, abusive behavior, or other traumatic occurrences. As in any crisis situation, the immediate needs of the family, especially the most vulnerable members, must be attended to before long-term changes can be pursued. Although the therapist occasionally must serve as a "Bandaid" for a family, this role should not be maintained for several sessions. Don't assume the role of "family rescuer." Help the family become aware of its abilities to work through times of crisis and to develop behavior for coping with future problems.

The Therapist's Self-maintenance

When your car begins to knock and clang, you don't hesitate to take it in for a tune-up. Like a car, a therapist's most important tool, himself, requires continuing evaluation and attention to remain at a high level and checkups should be ongoing. It is important for a therapist to take a look at himself on a regular basis. To begin, the therapist should take out a mirror, look at himself, and reflect on whether the following attributes are "in tune."

1. You feel that it's okay to be who you are, and you are willing to share yourself and what you do with other people.

2. You accept a *reasonable* standard of performance as being adequate. Understanding how an effective therapist acts and reacts, you prepare as necessary for a session, feel comfortable in the session, and do the best you can with the tools with which you have to work. You accept as inevitable the fact that you will make some mistakes, but after learning what you can from an experience, you are able to turn your thoughts and attentions to other things.

Acceptance of your performance as a therapist does not prevent you from considering changes in your approaches with a family. Rather than giving in to discouragement and self-blame, you look at your process in engaging families and make whatever changes seem necessary without self-recrimination.

3. You work within a comfortable time frame in your therapy sessions, and provide enough time to help a family experience constructive interactions. This should include taking time to think about the family before a session and to consider some appropriate types of intervention to help them move toward your mutual goals. It also means taking time after a session to think about what occurred and to formulate some tentative ideas for future contacts with the family.

4. You give high priority to having your own intimacy needs met. If you sense deficiencies in this area, you take time to enhance the support relationships that already exist in your life or work on developing new ones. The authors strongly agree with the point made by Luthman and Kirschenbaum (1974) that the degree of intimacy a family will pursue toward its growth in therapy is determined by the degree of intimacy with which the therapist himself is comfortable. When it comes to building a relationship, the therapist cannot take people where he himself has not been.

The Challenge To Become

The techniques that have been explored here for helping families can come to life only through a therapist's energy, skills, and desire. Experiences and techniques can be shared, but it is the therapist who gives them meaning and vitality.

You are the lifeblood of the therapy experience. Your gift of self, your unique nature, is what removes the mystery from the therapeutic relationship. You make real what is unreal and clarify that which is unclear in a manner that no one else can duplicate. No one has your personality or physical attributes, your way of relating to others. You radiate an exquisite color and warmth that is solely yours. You are an individual segment of an artistic design, with each component of complimentary hues blending together in kaleidoscopic collusion. You are in the process of growing and developing as you strive to become a family therapist.

Becoming a family therapist begins with a belief in yourself as a capable, compassionate human being and an awareness of the interrelationship between an individual family member's behavior and a family's interactions. Before you is the challenge to integrate techniques into your personal repertoire and utilize them to help free the family from its painful interactions.

Before you is the challenge to become.

References

Ackerman, N., Beatman, F., & Sherman, S. (Eds.). *Exploring the base for family therapy*. New York: Family Service Association of America, 1961.

Bandler, R., Grinder, J., & Satir, V. *Changing with families*. Palo Alto, Calif.: Science & Behavior Books, 1976.

Bateson, G., Jackson, D., Haley, J., & Weakland, J. Toward a theory of schizophrenia. *Behavioral Science*, 1956, *1*, 251–64.

Beier, E., Robinson, P., & Micheletti, G. A community helps itself in mobilization of community resources of self-help in mental health. *Journal of Consulting Psychology*, 1971, *36*, 142–250.

Bloch, D. A. (Ed.). *Primer of family therapy*. New York: Grune & Stratton, 1973.

Bloch, D. A. (Ed.). *Techniques of family psychotherapy: A primer*. New York: Grune & Stratton, 1973.

Bowen, M. *Family therapy in clinical practice*. New York: Jason Aronson, 1978.

Dodson, L. *Family counseling: A systems approach*. Muncie: Accelerated Development, 1977.

Framo, J. L. Family of origin as a therapeutic resource for adults in marital and family therapy: You can and should go home again. *Family Process*, 1976, *15*, 193–210.

Geismar, L. L., & Ayres, B. *Patterns of change in problem families*. St. Paul: Family Centered Project of the Greater St. Paul Community Chest and Council, 1959.

Guerin, P. J. (Ed.). *Family Therapy*. New York: Gardner Press, 1976.

Gurman, A., & Kniskern, D. Deterioration in marital and family therapy: Empirical, clinical, and conceptual issues. *Family Process*. 1978, *17*, 3–20.

Gurman, A., & Kniskern, D. (Ed.). *Handbook of family therapy*. New York: Brunner/Mazel, 1981.

Haley, J. *Problem solving therapy*. San Francisco: Jossey-Bass, 1977.

Headley, L. *Adults and their parents in family therapy*. New York: Plenum, 1977.

Herr, J. J., & Weakland, J. H. *Counseling elders and their families*. New York: Springer Publishing, 1979.

Jones, N., Neuman, R., & Shyne, A. *A second chance for families; Evalua-*

tion of a program to reduce foster care. New York: Child Welfare League of America, 1976.

Koch, J., & Koch, L. *The marriage savers.* New York: Coward, McCann & Geoghegan, 1976.

Langsley, D., & Kaplan, D. *The treatment of families in crisis.* New York: Grune & Stratton, 1968.

Lederer, W. J., & Jackson, D. D. *The mirages of marriage.* New York: W. W. Norton, 1968.

Leveton, E. *Children in trouble: Families in crisis.* Davis: Center on Administration of Criminal Justice, University of California, 1976.

Leveton, E. *Psychodrama for the timid clinician.* New York: Springer Publishing, 1977.

Lutham, S. G., & Kirschenbaum, M. *The dynamic family.* Palo Alto, Calif.: Science & Behavior Books, 1974.

Lynch, C., The freedom to get mad: Impediments to expressing anger and how to deal with them. *Family Therapy,* 2, 101–122. 1975,

Minuchin, S. *Families and family therapy.* Cambridge, Mass.: Harvard University Press, 1974.

Napier, A., & Whitaker, C. *The family crucible.* New York: Harper & Row, 1978.

Olson, D. *Treating relationships.* Lake Mills, Iowa: Graphic Publishing, 1976.

Paul, N. The role of mourning and empathy in conjoint marital therapy. In G. Zuk & I. Boszormenyi-Nagy (Eds.), *Family therapy and disturbed families.* Palo Alto, Calif.: Science and Behavior Books, 1967.

Paul, N., & Paul, B. *A marital puzzle.* New York: Norton, 1975.

Pittman, F. *Unconventional intervention with difficult families.* Paper presented at the meeting of the American Orthopsychiatric Association, San Francisco, March 1978.

Roberts, R. Treating conduct disordered adolescents and young adults by working with their parents. *Journal of Marital and Family Therapy,* 1982, 8, 15–28.

Satir, V. *Conjoint family therapy* (rev. ed.). Palo Alto, Calif.: Science and Behavior Books, 1967.

Satir, V. *Peoplemaking.* Palo Alto, Calif.: Science and Behavior Books, 1972.

Satir, V., Stachowiak, J., & Taschman, H. A. *Helping families to change.* New York: Jason Aronson, 1975.

Sharp, L., & Lantz, J. Relabeling in conjoint family therapy. *Journal of Psychiatric Nursing and Mental Health Services,* 1978, 16, 29–33.

Visher, E. B., & John, S. *Step-families.* New York: Brunner/Mazel, 1979.

Watzlawick, P. A structured family interview. *Family Process,* 1966, 5, 256–271.

Watzlawick, P. *The language of change.* New York: Basic Books, 1978.
Watzlawick, P., Weakland, J., & Fisch, R. *Change.* New York: W. W. Norton, 1974.
Williamson, D. Personal authority in family experience via termination of the intergenerational hierarchial boundary. *Journal of Marital and Family Therapy,* 1982, *8,* 309–323.
Zuk, G. *Family therapy: A triadic-based approach.* New York: Behavioral Publications, 1971.

Appendix: Improving Family Therapy Skills

The beginning therapist should seek the help of an experienced family therapist, when one is available, to improve his therapy skills. The *Directory of Clinical Members and Approved Supervisors* of the American Association for Marriage and Family Therapy, 1717 K Street NW, #407, Washington, D.C., 20006, is a good resource for locating experienced therapists. Gaining experience in the use of effective intervention tools with families might be arranged in several ways.

An experienced therapist may be asked to critique a beginner's work with families and to offer suggestions by reviewing audio- or videotaped family sessions that the beginning therapist has done. Always get the family's permission in advance. The experienced therapist may also be asked to observe and critique the new therapist's work in family interviews by using a one-way observation glass. Again, the family's prior permission is required. In some training programs, telephones are used in the interviewing room with the supervisor calling observations in to the new therapist during the session. The supervisor also might come into a session and participate with the student during particularly difficult segments of an interview. A helpful article entitled "Through the Looking Glass: Supervision in Family Therapy" in the March 1978 issue of *Social Casework* may be useful in understanding this process further.

The experienced therapist can also be of help by allowing the beginner to observe him in his work with families, and by discussing the beginning therapist's observations following the session. Observations can be made by viewing and/or listening to audio- or videotapes of the experienced therapist's family session, observing his work through a one-way observation glass, or serving as a co-therapist in a family interview.

Unfortunately, the opportunity to work with experienced family therapists is not always available, particularly in rural areas. But increasing skills through a variety of learning experiences in such settings is possible. Several recommended experiences include reading some of the many excellent books and periodicals on family therapy. Many of these resources are included in the "Additional Readings" at the end of this book. Observing and discussing, ideally with other beginning family therapists, audio- and videotapes and films of family interviews done by experienced family therapists is also recommended.

1. The five one-hour training films (*Family Process, Family Rules, Experiential Techniques, Use of Self, and Demonstration of a Counseling Session: Candy*) done by Alan and Eva Leveton of the Family Therapy Institute of San Francisco are strongly recommended. These are available through:

The National Criminal Justice Reference Service, P.O. Box 24036, Southwest Station, Washington, D.C. 20024.

2. Two excellent sources for attaining videotapes are:

Georgetown Family Center, 4380 MacArthur Boulevard N.W., Washington, D.C. 20007.

Strategic Therapy Training Center, 4602 North Park Avenue, Chevy Chase, MD 20815.

3. Other family therapy films and video tapes are available through these sources:

Science and Behavior Books, P.O. Box 11457, Palo Alto, California 94306.

Continuing Education Media, Eastern Pennsylvania Psychiatric Institute, Henry Avenue and Abbottsford Road, Philadelphia, PA 19129.

Philadelphia Child Guidance Clinic, Two Children's Center, 34th St. and Civic Center Boulevard, Philadelphia, PA 19104

Nathan W. Ackerman Family Institute, 149 East 78th Street, New York, N.Y. 10021.

The Boston Family Institute, 251 Harvard Square, Brookline, Mass. 02146.

The Family Studies Section, Bronx State Hospital, 1500 Waters Place, Bronx, NY 10461.

4. Another excellent source is:

School of Social Work Media Center, University of Wisconsin, 425 Henry Mall, Madison, WI 53706.

An additional resource may be the film libraries of major colleges and universities, or the audiovisual library of a state division of Human Resources or Health and Social Services.

Making audio- or videotapes of family interviews and critiquing them alone or with other family therapy learners is another good learning technique. The following questions may be helpful to consider in such critiques.

What were the goals for this session?

What interventions were used to reach them and how did they work?

In general, how successful did you as the therapist feel you were in reaching the goals established for the session? In areas where you experienced little or no success, can you think of any alternative interventions you might have tried?

What goals do you hope to reach in future work with this family?

In role-playing with other family therapy learners, it is especially helpful to ask one member of the group to choose a family with which he is working or has worked in the past. That member is asked to set up a simulation of the family, using members from the group to play the roles of family members. The individual presenting the family should take a key family role. After roles have been established, one or two people in the group are asked to take the role of a family therapist and to conduct a session with the family. The main purpose of the session is to identify and help the family begin working on some of its concerns. Following the session, a critique session involving the entire group is held, using this format.

Check with the "therapists" to find out:

How they experienced the session.

How they experienced working with each other.

What they were trying to accomplish in the session.

Why they used particular kinds of interventions.

What they did with the family that they felt positive about.

What they did that in retrospect they might have done differently.

If they were to continue working with the family, what their goals might be in the future sessions.

Next check with the "family" to find out:

> How they experienced the session.
> What the therapists did that they found helpful and why it was helpful.
> What the therapists might have done differently.

Finally, talk with others observing the session to learn what interventions they thought were helpful, and whether they have any suggestions for other interventions the therapists might have used.

Additional Readings

Ables, B., & Brandsma, J. *Therapy for couples.* San Francisco: Jossey-Bass, 1977.

Ackerman, N., et al. *Exploring the base for family therapy.* Family Service Association of America, 1961.

Ackerman, N. (Ed.). *Family Process.* New York: Basic Books, 1970.

Ackerman, N. *The psychodynamics of family life.* New York: Basic Books, 1958.

Ackerman, N. *Treating the troubled family.* New York: Basic Books, 1966.

Andrews, E. *The emotionally disturbed family.* New York: Jason Aronson, 1974.

Ard, B., & Ard, C. *Handbook of marriage counseling.* Palo Alto, Calif.: Science and Behavior Books, 1966.

Bane, M. *Here to stay: American families in the 20th century.* New York: Basic Books, 1976.

Beavers, R. *Psychotherapy & growth: A family systems perspective.* New York: Brunner/Mazel, 1977.

Beier, E. G. *The silent language of psychotherapy.* Chicago: Aldine Publishing, 1966.

Berenson, G., & White, H. *Annual review of family therapy.* New York: Human Sciences Press, 1981.

Boszormenyi-Nagy, T., & Framo, J. (Eds.). *Intensive family therapy.* New York: Harper & Row, 1965.

Carter, E. A., & Orfanidis, M. M. (Eds.). *The family life cycle.* New York: Gardner, 1980.

Clinebell, C., & Clinebell, H., *The intimate marriage.* New York: Harper & Row, 1970.

Couch, E. *Joint & family interviews in the treatment of marital problems.* New York: Family Service Association of America, 1969.

Dreikurs, R., Corsini, L., & Sonstegard, M. (Eds.). *Adlerian family counseling: A manual for counseling centers.* Eugene: University of Oregon Press, 1959.

Eisentein, V., *Neurotic interaction in marriage.* New York: Basic Books, 1958.

Ferber, A., Mendelsohn, M., & Napier, A. (Eds.). *The book of family therapy.* New York: Jason Aronson, 1972.

Foley, V. *An introduction to family therapy.* New York: Grune & Stratton, 1980.

Forward, S., & Buck, C. *Betrayal of innocence: Incest & its devastation.* New York: Tracher/St. Martin's, 1978.

Framo, J. (Ed.). *Family interaction.* New York: Springer Publishing, 1972.

Garland, D. *Couples' communications and negotiation skills.* New York: Family Service Association, 1973.

Geismar, L. L., & Ayers, B. *Measuring family functioning.* St. Paul: Greater St. Paul Community Chest & Councils, 1957.

Glick, I., & Kessler, D. *Marital and family therapy.* New York: Grune & Stratton, 1980.

Green, B. (Ed.). *The psychotherapies of marital disharmony.* New York: The Free Press, 1965.

Guerny, B. *Relationship enhancement.* San Francisco: Jossey-Bass, 1977.

Gurman, A. (Ed.). *Questions and answers in the practice of family therapy.* New York: Brunner/Mazel, 1981.

Gurman, A., & Rice, D. G., *Couples in conflict.* New York: Jason Aronson, 1975.

Haley, J., & Hoffman, L. (Eds.). *Techniques of family therapy.* New York: Basic Books, 1967.

Haley, J. *Changing families: A family therapy reader.* New York: Grune & Stratton, 1971.

Haley, J. *Leaving home.* New York: McGraw/Hill, 1980.

Haley, J. *Strategies of psychotherapy.* New York: Grune & Stratton, 1963.

Haley, J. *Uncommon therapy.* New York: W. W. Norton, 1973.

Herr, J., & Weakland, J. *Counseling elders and their families.* Springer, 1979.

Hoffman, L. *Foundation of family therapy.* New York: Basic Books, 1981.

Hollingsworth, C., & Pasnau, R. *The family in mourning.* New York: Grune & Stratton, 1976.

Horne, A., & Ohlsen, M. *Family counseling and therapy.* Itasca, Ill.: Peacock, 1982.

Jones, S. *Family therapy: A comparison of approaches.* Bowie, Maryl.: Robert J. Brady, 1980.

Kantor, D., & Lehr, W. *Inside the family.* San Francisco: Jossey-Bass, 1975.

Kaplan, H. *The new sex therapy.* New York: Brunner/Mazel, 1974.

Kaufmann, E., & Kaufmann, P. (Eds.). *Family therapy of drug and alcohol abusers: From enmeshed enemy to ally.* New York: Gardner, 1982.

Knox, D. *Marriage happiness.* Champaign, Ill.: Research Press, 1971.

L'Abate, L. *Understanding and helping the individual in the family.* New York: Grune & Stratton, 1976.

Lasswell, M., & Lobsenz, N. *No-fault marriage.* Garden City: Doubleday, 1976.

Levinger, G., & Moles, O. (Eds.). *Divorce and separation.* New York: Basic Books, 1979.

Lewis, J., Beavers, W., Gossett, J., & Phillips, U. *No single thread.* New York: Brunner/Mazel, 1976.

Lobsenz, N., & Blackburn, C. *How to stay married.* New York: Family Service Association, 1968.

Madanes, C. *Strategic Family Therapy.* San Francisco: Jossey-Bass, 1981.

Martin, P. A. *Marital therapy manual.* New York: Brunner/Mazel, 1976.

Masters, W., Johnson, V., & Kolodny, R. (Eds.). *Ethical issues in sex therapy and research.* Boston: Little, Brown, 1977.

Mayleas, D. *Rewedded bliss.* New York: Basic Books, 1979.

Minuchin, S. *Families and family therapy.* Cambridge: Harvard University Press, 1974.

Minuchin, S. *Families of the slum.* Cambridge: Harvard University Press, 1967.

Minuchin, S., Fishman, C. *Family therapy techniques.* Cambridge: Harvard University Press, 1981.

Minuchin, S., Rosman, B., & Baker, L. *Psychosomatic families.* Cambridge: Harvard University Press, 1978.

Mostwin, D. *Special dimensions of family treatment.* Washington, D.C.: National Association of Social Workers, 1980.

Munson, C. *Social work with families.* New York: The Free Press, 1980.

Olson, D. H. (Ed.). *Treating relationships.* Lake Mills, Iowa: Graphic Publishing Co., 1976.

Palazzoli, M., Boscolo, L., Cecchin, G., & Prata, G. *Paradox & Counterparadox.* New York: Jason Aronson, 1978.

Papajohn, J., & Spiegel, J. *Transactions in families.* San Francisco: Jossey-Bass, 1974.

Papp, P. (Ed.). *Family therapy: Full-length case studies.* New York: Halstead, 1978.

Patterson, G. *Families.* Champaign, Ill.: Research Press, 1971.

Pearce, J., & Friedman, L. (Eds.). *Family therapy.* New York: Grune & Stratton, 1980.

Peck, B. *A family therapy notebook.* Roslyn Heights, N.Y.: Libra, 1974.

Rogers, C. *Becoming partners.* New York: Delacorte, 1972.

Satir, V. *Peoplemaking.* Palo Alto, Calif.: Science and Behavior Books, 1972.

Satir, V. *Conjoint family therapy.* Palo Alto, Calif.: Science & Behavior Books, 1967.

Satir, V., Stachowick, J., & Taschman, H. *Helping families to change.* New York: Jason Aronson, 1976.

Skynner, A. C. *Systems of family and marital psychotherapy.* New York: Brunner/Mazel, 1976.

Stanton, M. D., Todd, T. C., et al. *The family therapy of drug abuse and addiction.* New York: Guilford, 1982.

Stierlin, H., Rucker-Embden, I., Wezel, N., & Wirsching, M. *The first interview*. New York: Brunner/Mazel, 1981.

Tinker, K. *Let's look at our failures*. St. Paul: Greater St. Paul Community Chest & Councils, 1957.

Visher, E., & Visher, J. *Step-families*. New York: Brunner/Mazel, 1979.

Voiland, A. *Family casework diagnosis*. New York: Columbia University Press, 1962.

Wald, E. *The remarried family: Challenge and promise*. New York: Family Service Association, 1978.

Walsh, N. (Ed.). *Normal family processes*. New York: Guilford, 1982.

Walz, G., & Benjamin, L. *Transcultural counseling: Needs, programs and techniques*. New York: Human Sciences, 1978.

Watzlawick, P. *How real is real? Confusion, disinformation, communication*. New York: Random House, 1976.

Watzlawick, P., & Weakland, J. (Eds.). *The interactional view*. New York: W. W. Norton, 1977.

Wegscheider, S. *Another chance: Hope and health for the alcoholic family*. Palo Alto, Calif.: Behavior Books, 1981.

JOURNALS

The American Journal of Family Therapy - 19 Union Sq. W. - New York 10003

Marriage and Family Review - 28 East 22nd St. - New York 10010

The Family Coordinator - 1219 University Ave. S.E. - Minneapolis, MN 55414

Family Process - 149 E. 78th St. - New York 10021

Family Therapy - 321 Wilets Rd., Roslyn Heights, N.Y. 11577

Family Therapy Networker - 2334 Cedar Lane - Vienna, Va. 22180

International Journal of Family Therapy - 72 Fifth Ave. - New York 10011

Journal of Marital and Family Therapy - 1717 K. St. N.W. #407 - Washington, D.C. 20006

Journal of Marriage & the Family - 1219 University Ave. S.E., Minneapolis, MN 10021

Index